50 YEARS OF

50 Years
of Service

O. G. GORING

LONDON
THE GORING HOTEL

*The First Hotel in the
World with a Private
Bathroom to every Bedroom.*

CONTENTS

Souvenir panel faced by its key, page 128

Pages from the Visitors' Book between pages 128 and 129

This photograph of George Goring was taken for the *New York Times* in 1983 to illustrate George's policy of trying out all his bedrooms by sleeping in them personally. For many years The Goring did not pay commission to Agents — for this reason it was known throughout America as "The Boring Goring" — hence the proposed theme adopted by the *New York Times* — Boring Old George "sleeps around".

Introduction to the Third Edition

EIGHT eventful years have passed since I wrote the 1976 introduction to my father's book which now reprints again. I am convinced that the secret of our continued success at The Goring has been our ability to maintain the management style and fundamental principles outlined in that introduction, which I have included in this 1984 edition.

William Cowpe has been General Manager of the hotel for twelve years and has a growing family of his own. Two Goring boys are at present attending Hotel School prior to going abroad for a few years' fundamental training. Hopefully they will then maintain our tradition of always having a Mr. Goring at The Goring, to greet the families of our present generation of patrons.

Thelma Fabian (Head Receptionist) retired in 1980 after 25 years. Leslie Nicol (Head Hall Porter) retired in 1982 after 49 years and is now thoroughly enjoying himself as Secretary of the internationally esteemed *Societe des Clefs d'Or*.

Tony Perilli (Head Waiter) since 1938 has just retired and married my Father's ex-Secretary, Betty Simpson, and they are now living happily at Knaresborough. Miss Simpson's successor in 1952, Edwina Davy, has bravely stayed on as my Personal Secretary to this day. The same tradition has been continued by Mary Scoggins who now assists William Cowpe, previously having been Norman Pennington's Secretary from 1956 to 1970.

Many of the old faces still remain — Peter Sweeney (Doorman) since 1965 and Eddie Fantela (Larder Cook) since 1955, along with some very welcome fairly new faces:

Paul Keegan (Food and Beverage Manager) since 1980
Deter Sondermann (Chef) since 1978
Mary Davin (Head Housekeeper) since 1975
Doris Dickson (Head Receptionist) since 1979
Frank Lopez (Head Hall Porter) since 1979
Ernest De Blasi (Head Hall Porter) since 1975

We now employ 125 staff at The Goring, only fifteen of whom have been with us for less than a year.

The London hotel scene has become very competitive and more volatile since 1976 but I think you will agree that The Goring has more than kept pace with developments. We have streamlined and computerised our telephone, telex and Reception accounting systems. I cannot think of a relevant bedroom appliance or accessory that all our bedrooms do not include. I make a practice, whenever possible, to sleep a night in each individual bedroom on their becoming vacant, and am certain that our standards of cleanliness and decoration are second to none. Every year we spend a quarter of a million pounds (15% of turnover) on redecorating and enhancing our bedrooms, private suites, lounges, dining rooms etc.

Running a hotel is great fun and very exciting. I am reminded, when looking through recent signatures in our Visitor's Book, that not all well known or distinguished visitors to London prefer to stay in large "flashy" hotels operated by international conglomerates. There are many such people who prefer to stay in a quieter style of hotel and who do not wish to advertise their whereabouts. I note the names of three out of the past four Prime Ministers, two Chancellors of the Exchequer, and no less than fifteen recent Cabinet Ministers, amongst a most interesting list of Heads of Industry, Royalty, Union Leaders and Sporting Personalities.

Britain is a civilised and very lovely country. At The Goring we consider ourselves specially fortunate and privileged to be able to welcome so many interesting guests from all over the world to our family home.

GEORGE GORING

Introduction to the Second Edition

A VERY successful sixteen years have passed by since my father wrote this book for our Golden Jubilee in 1960 and, as it has now become necessary to reprint, I am taking the opportunity to bring you up to date.

Apart from numerous modernisation schemes, which have successfully improved the amenities and comfort of the hotel for our guests, we remain essentially unaltered.

A grading scheme has now been introduced into London Hotels and we have been awarded Four Red Stars which indicates that we, along with three other hotels, are the best in our category in London.

Government legislation has completely changed the face of the hotel industry, and it has been said that The Goring Hotel stands out as one of the last bastions of private enterprise left in London.

We still like to feel that our many friends from all over the world can regard us as a 'home from home' on the occasions when they visit us. We do not have the assistance of large marketing consortia, or monopolies, to project our image, but we do have the advantage, as a family concern, of being able to treat our guests and staff as human beings.

Inevitably some of the dear old faces have disappeared from amongst our members of staff. Mr. Norman Pennington died of cancer at the age of fifty-seven in 1970, leaving us all wondering how on earth we were going to manage without him. Many of our older and longer serving staff have retired and some of their replacements have already been with us for many years. I am now thirty-seven years of age and several employees still remember my being born, a fact which I found distinctly embarrassing when I came back from abroad to start work under Mr. Pennington in December 1961. It is very hard to discipline somebody who has actually helped my mother to cope with me during my infancy.

In November 1974 my father died after a long illness. We all miss the benefit of his experience and feel that the industry has lost a great character.

What does the future hold in store for us? I feel confident that, in spite of enormous pressures being brought to bear by Government, Agents, Unions, and large monopolies, there will still be a place in our society for The Goring Hotel and all that we stand for.

GEORGE GORING

Foreword

SOME twenty-five years ago Mr. Sinclair Lewis, the great American author, wrote a book which I thought was a most sensitive study of the life of a would-be aspirant to our industry.

This young man, born and brought up in his parents' small hotel in a small town in America, feels he has a flair for the business, but is dubious about going into it for reasons which, of course, you all know so well.

He confides his doubts to an old commercial traveller, and God knows they are the greatest authorities on hotels ever. The commercial traveller tells him of the importance of hotels and the greatness of the future of this trade, but he feels he should make it fairly clear to him just what it means, just what he has got to do to become an hotelier, and he says to him, and here I quote:

'You will have to learn manners, learn to be poker-faced with people that would take advantage of you. You will have to know all about china and silver, glass, linen, brocades, and the best woods for flooring and furniture.

'A hotel manager has to be a combination of a *hausfrau*; a chef; a bar-room bouncer; a doctor for emergencies; a wetnurse; a lawyer that knows more about the rights and wrongs of guests and how far he dare go than old man Supreme Court himself; an upholsterer; a walking directory that knows off-hand without looking it up just where the Hardshell Baptist Church is, what time the marriage licence bureau opens, and what time the local starts for Hick Junction.

'He's got to be a certified accountant; a professor of languages; a quick-action laundry man; a plumber; a heating engineer; a carpenter; a swell speech-maker; an authority on the importance of every tinhorn state Senator or one-night-stand lecturer that blows in and expects to have the red carpet already hauled out for him; a fly cop that can tell from looking at a girl's ears whether she's married to the guy or not; a money-lender, only he doesn't get any interest or have any security.

'He's got to be dressed better than a Twenty-third Street actor, even if he has nothing in his pocket. He's got to be able, just from hearing a cow's moo, to tell whether she will make good steaks.

'He's got to know more about wine and cigars than the fellas that make them. They can fool around and try experiments, but he's got to sell them.

'All the time he's got to be a diplomat that would make Thomas Beyard look like John L. Sullivan on a spree. He's got to set a table like a Vanderbilt, yet watch the pennies like an Arab pedlar.

'If you can do all this you'll have a good time. Go to it. . . .'

Preface

WE are all proud to reach our golden jubilee in a business which has flourished. This can truly be said of the Goring.

Opened on 1st March, 1910, by my father, Mr. O. R. Goring, the first visitor took up occupancy on my birthday, 2nd March, 1910.

The hotel has never looked back. Three extensions were built before 1926, and since then the internal economy has been so greatly improved, both in rentability and in equipment, that the premises have for many years now worked to maximum capacity. The percentages shown below have often staggered me.

Unlike other industries, maximum capacity in hotels stops with the capacity of the structure. Yet year after year since 1945 the Goring Hotel has shown increased turnover in all departments from approximately 60 per cent. of turnover in 1939 to nearly 97 per cent. from 1950 onwards.

One has no means of assessing—except very roughly—one's actual standing in one's own industry, except by financial gain. In the hotel world, however, financial gain, if taken to extremes, can be, and often is, a sign of decay. To put back a lot of what you take out is a sound doctrine.

One of the most difficult problems in hotel-keeping is the constant attention to detail.

By good fortune, and possibly good management, the Goring has retained its staff over the years to such effect that they are always present to welcome the returning guest. Many of the staff I engaged as young men way back after the First World War. Do not think that they are thus 'old men'. They are not. They are in the prime of life.

Mr. W. N. Pennington, my Manager, who has stood by me so loyally and efficiently all these years, came to me in quite a junior position in 1938. After a brilliant war record from

private soldier to acting Colonel, he has been my right-hand
man ever since.

*

My father took the bold step of naming the Goring Hotel
after himself—never thinking of the illustrious future. For
many years now (since 1924, when I became Manager) I have
had the distinction of using my name in connection with it.

Psychologically this is by far the best way of hotel management—Mr. Goring of the Goring Hotel.

Gone are the days of César Ritz of the Ritz; Mr. Claridge
of Claridge's, Mr. Brown of Brown's, Mr. Long of Long's,
Mr. Symond of Symond's, Mr. White of White's, and
Mr. Morley of Morley's. In other words, gone are the days
of the individual 'mine host'.

I know from thousands of conversations that the personal
name has helped my business—for the hotel business thrives
on personality towards the public.

That is why the Goring Hotel has never exceeded 100
bedrooms. Once an establishment 'reaches out', it loses a lot
of its individuality—not only in management, but also in staff
organization. Large establishments may have super-efficient
checks and controls, but they cannot compete in staff-selection.
In other words, their staff needs are so much greater that they
must have a much higher percentage of inferior employees.
None of us can expect to reach and keep 100 per cent., but we
can get quite near it in the smaller hotel.

For myself and family, individuality is a good thing. While
presenting an overwhelming feeling of responsibility which
can be mentally wearing at times, it nevertheless urges one on
'for the good of the name'.

So many firms today hide individuality behind long titles,
giving no insight of the personalities operating them, and no
indication to the general public as to how and when these
individuals come and go.

                                    O. G. GORING, F.H.C.I.

My Father

So many visitors look at the photograph of my father, Mr. O. R. Goring, which hangs in the front hall of the hotel, and recognize him as the genial 'mine host' of between the wars, that I have tried to recollect some of the salient points in his life.

He was born in Schleitz, on a farm in a small farming village in southern Saxony, of German parents.

His name was Göring (pronounced Goering)—a very unusual name in Germany—and in fact almost unique until it was made world-famous by a character in the last war. The name means the 'King's pike-bearer'. So far as I am aware, there is only one main family of Gorings in England—namely, the Gorings who own Goring-by-Sea, near Worthing in Sussex. This family dates back a very long way in our history, and has always had distinguished sons and daughters, prominent in public service.

Today, however, there are a lot of people of the name of Goring. In the past the London telephone directory listed about five people of that name. Now there is over half a column. Many of these people are refugees from Europe and reached here between the wars, changing their names by deed-poll. I have noticed, however, that this practice stopped within a year or two of Hitler's coming into power.

In the time of Edward III there was a corps of the King's pike-bearers—mercenaries from one of the small German states of those days—known locally as 'the Goeringers'. This German name became corrupted—or, rather, altered—with the years, the Sussex pronunciation becoming 'Goring' and the Kent pronunciation 'Geering'. These changes in pronunciation fit in exactly with the dialect of both counties. In fact, there is still a firm of Geering and Collyer in Maidstone. Mr. Geering explained the above details to me with much pride.

On my family's side it is known that an English officer of the name of Goring followed Napoleon on the way to Moscow in 1812. He was badly injured either by fighting or frostbite, and had his leg amputated. He is also known to have settled in Schleitz, and married there.

So perhaps my father was only coming back again to England after two generations in Europe.

Apparently his parents left the countryside and settled in Meissen, near Dresden, the home of the famous Dresden China Factory. Here my grandfather would appear to have had a mixed coal and wood agency, and also a mineral-water-bottling plant. This is hearsay, for I was born after he died.

My father had two younger brothers, Alwin and Bernhardt. Bernhardt, the youngest, joined the Dresden China Factory and made his name as a painter on china. His speciality was the white china painted with small flowers—forget-me-nots, roses, crocuses, pansies, ferns, etc.—which was so fashionable at the turn of the century and which commands such high prices today. For many years up to about 1925 he was head of that department, until he went into production on his own.

I still have a number of his paintings—motifs of small flower posies painted on blank postcards and sent to me and my mother every birthday, Easter and Christmas. I saw him paint one once—it took under five minutes, so used was he to his work. Transfer work was not accepted then in his department of the factory.

My father never took to his own father's agency. He wanted to get into the hotel business, and so did his younger brother, Alwin.

They appear to have left home to seek their fortunes. My father went to Weimar, to the best hotel there, to serve as a waiter. During his period there he had the honour to serve the Crown Prince of Germany, who was staying in the hotel. One evening the Crown Prince gave a dinner party in a room overlooking a balcony decked in geraniums. The season was June—strawberry time—and the Prince ordered the well-known German drink of champagne cup with cucumber and fresh strawberries. Things went merrily with his party of forty, and many strawberry cups were consumed.

The waiters behind the scenes also had more than their fair share, it would appear. My father went to bed in his room at the top of the hotel and was violently sick out of the window! Next morning, on laying up breakfast in the Crown Prince's suite, he was flabbergasted to see that he had been ill from above all over the plants on the Prince's balcony. The Prince came in. 'Yes, young man, I have already noticed that the geraniums have grown strawberries since last night', he said.

A year later, at about the turn of the 1890s, my father was working as a waiter at the famous old Frankfurterhof in Frankfurt, visiting-ground of all European royalty in those days when every country was ruled by a king or emperor.

King Edward VII was there at the time, and came down to his usual table at breakfast one morning. Another gentleman followed a few minutes later, and my father, as only a junior waiter, placed him at the same table. The restaurant Manager, on seeing this, became absolutely livid and could hardly speak for rage.

'Young idiot, what the devil have you done now?' he demanded.

My father replied quietly: 'Nothing—except to place the King of Bulgaria at the same table as his cousin, King Edward VII.'

London has always been the Mecca of the enterprising hoteliers from all parts of Europe, and no well-known hotel manager has not spent some time in our capital city. As I travelled round Europe—both before and after the war—I was met daily by my friends: 'When I was at the Piccadilly Hotel in 1897', 'When I was a waiter at the Savoy in 1908,' 'When I was at the Hotel Cecil in 1909,' etc. Those, of course, were the days of no passports or work permits. Everyone was free to go where he or she wished, and the most enterprising won.

Russia was the only exception.

That is why the first-class London hotels even today are of such a high standard. I know, because I have visited most of the best hotels in Europe and have experienced their good points and their defects. Until comparatively recently they could employ international staff.

In any case, Mr. O. R. Goring came to London about 1893, and started as an extra waiter at the Hotel Metropole, being employed each evening on banquet duties. Those were the days of nine-course meals with entertainment, and the late hours did not matter—except to the waiters. In those days one was engaged by an employment agency run by a German of the name of Boden. He also had an important agency for Schlesinger of Berlin, who made shirts. Obviously, to get a job it was tactful to buy a shirt. If one had no money, this was done on credit. I can just remember little Boden—one of those comic characters, entirely round, with a bald head, whom our cartoonists delight in, 'Pop-like' in aspect.

My father continued to buy his shirts from Boden up to 1914, so that is how I got to see him. Incidentally, the shirts were extremely good ones. Little Boden was interned in 1915.

Boden used to line up his team of extra waiters at 6.30 p.m. in any hotel where he happened to have a team working. He went through them like a parade sergeant—clean white gloves, clean shirt and cuffs, hair-cut, clean finger-nails not stained with nicotine (although they wore gloves!), clean boots, etc. The men resented it in some cases, but if they did not conform they were not re-employed by Boden. And Boden, with his super-smart teams of waiters, commanded the attention of the managements. Boden's men, in fact, commanded a fee of 7s. 6d. per night up to 2-3 a.m., against 6s. 6d. elsewhere.

Many a rainy or foggy morning, my father, tired out, stumbled across Hungerford Bridge to his lodging room in the early hours.

On one such evening—it was Christmas Eve, and the work had been particularly hard—he returned to find his room burnt out and himself clotheless and penniless. He never got over it, and was always bad-tempered at Christmas until he died.

Those were the days of Mallaby-Deeley and Colonel North, with their gigantic property deals and fabulous champagne parties. Colonel North, who almost lived at the Hotel Metropole at the time, is said often to have danced on the dinner table as the hour grew late.

By the end of the century my father was managing a new

hotel of about fifty rooms at Westcliff-on-Sea, a suburb of Southend and about thirty miles from London.

The Queen's Hotel, with its beautiful gardens and conservatories, was very near the station, and soon became known to City men, who in many cases lived there.

My father married a Miss Alice Tracy in 1899, and he was naturalized in 1902. He always—quite rightly in my opinion—said that where a man was happy, was accepted into a country, made his money, paid his taxes, and married a woman of that country, it was his duty to become a citizen of that country.

I was born in Room No. 23 at the Queen's Hotel in 1901.

My Uncle Alwin came over as Chef in 1902—after being Head Pastry Chef at the big Central Hotel in Berlin for five years. The management formed a good team and business flourished.

Soon the hotel position at Southend changed, and while the Queen's Hotel remained the quieter one, my father also took over that great white elephant, the Palace Hotel, Southend (the same company)—for many years the biggest building in the town, and quite the most difficult to run. After many, many changes of management, it was sold out of the hotel business about two years ago, but its ugly, massive structure still forms a prominent landmark and can be seen from well out to sea at the mouth of the Thames.

The Queen's Hotel still exists, but many alterations have been made during the last half-century, and it now is a 'popular house', with a great deal of space devoted to bars.

By 1905 O. R. Goring was already in negotiation for the Naval and Military Club in the Harrington Road, South Kensington, a shabby building of several houses joined together by a corridor on the second floor. He bought out the Club, redecorated it, put in a lift, and opened it as the Harrington Hotel. He also got rid of most of the old residents, who were living there at about £2 per week *en pension*. With the opening up of London by the Underground Railway, inaugurated only a few years previously, many of the large mansions of the rich were transformed into hotels of medium class, frequented by retired naval and military people living on small pensions. The only notable person I remember was a Colonel Foss, who misguidedly had put his money into the still famous

Spanish galleon sunk in Tobermory Bay, said to contain many thousands of Spanish gold ducats, with which to pay the ill-fated Spanish Armada of 1588. The galleon is still at the bottom of Tobermory Bay and more than one syndicate has tried unsuccessfully to raise the gold since then.

The Harrington Hotel was not in my father's line, but he was at least his own proprietor, and it served as a stepping-stone to a successful entry into London.

Within two years he had acquired the Cromwell Hotel in Thurloe Place, opposite South Kensington Station, which he put under management.

The Harrington Hotel received a direct bomb hit in 1942, but the Cromwell Hotel still exists.

Ambitious, my father could not endure the eternal haggling over pennies with which his visitors—or, rather, residents—annoyed him. So when a site in Ebury Street became available he was far-seeing enough to acquire it and have the Goring Hotel built.

As we know, it was at once successful. He had chosen his site well, with a view to future development in the Victoria area, but he could not possibly have foreseen the tremendous change for the better in the Grosvenor Gardens and Grosvenor Place district of Westminster.

Neither could he have foreseen the importance of Victoria Station, then only partially built, and the move of terminal Continental traffic from Charing Cross to Victoria after the First World War.

A genial 'mine host', his somewhat portly figure of medium height, with rosy complexion, twinkling blue eyes, and ginger moustache, he had a habit of making friends easily, and was a good mixer. Evening after evening he would sit in the hotel lounge and talk to his guests.

When I came into the business in 1924 he was at his best. He knew everyone who visited the hotel, and had a host of friends amongst his many hotel acquaintances. His boon companions in the hotel business during the pre-1914-18 War years were all very well known and successful—all of whom had made their way up from the bottom.

There was Mr. G. Branchini, for many years General Manager of Claridge's, who later bought Almond's Hotel off Bond Street and ran it most successfully for titled people until 1941, when it was bombed, and Mr. Gustave Gelardi, the General Manager of Walsingham House, who later bought the Grand Hotel, Folkestone, and the Cadogan Hotel in Sloane Street, London. No one will remember Walsingham House. It was built by Lord Walsingham very early in the century on the site of the present Ritz Hotel. Copying the lines of the Albany, it was let in suites of two rooms to titled and distinguished people. Every bedroom had its private bathroom, except for servants' rooms—for in those times every gentleman had a valet or butler. Lord Walsingham sold to César Ritz, who pulled down the building after only a few years of existence and replaced it with an extravagantly built Ritz Hotel, in which he lost a fortune. In fact, it is only since the 1939-45 War that the Ritz, London, has paid its way, under the control of Sir Bracewell Smith. The other Ritz hotels in Paris, New York, and elsewhere followed.

César Ritz was for some years previously General Manager of the Savoy Hotel.

Madame Ritz is still alive, and now lives in comfortable retirement in her native Switzerland, where I saw her only a year or so ago.

Mr. Heim, General Manager of the Piccadilly Hotel up to 1914 and Mr. Judah, that great Manager of the Café Royal up to his death a decade ago, were frequent guests to our house in those days.

Mr. Theim, a great character of the early 1900s, who had hotel interests in Glasgow (I believe he owned the Windsor Hotel, long since demolished), was another friend. This unfortunate man had one of the most 'hard luck' stories I have ever heard.

Being successful in Glasgow, he built the Peebles Hydro, a palatial establishment of several hundred rooms in its own park, complete with 'cure' facilities, and equidistant from Edinburgh and Glasgow. Everything was in his favour—a new building, accessibility, and glorious countryside. The fire insurance on the furnished building fell out on a certain date, when the contractors handed it over to Mr. Theim, and he had made a reinsurance to start two days later.

On the one and only night the Hydro was not insured it was burnt down, and our good friend was ruined.

Peebles Hydro is still one of the very best hotels in Scotland, and has held this position ever since the new company took over the bankrupt one many years ago.

Amongst many others, Mr. Henri Prüger—a Hungarian— came very much into our lives. He was for some years General Manager of the Savoy Hotel, and was later made General Manager and adviser to the R.A.C. in Pall Mall, then being built, in about 1912. Mr. Prüger often came to our home with his plans and troubles and Father and he would spend long hours discussing them. One great obstacle to the building of the R.A.C. was the fact that an uncharted spring—or rivulet— had suddenly shown its presence when the foundations were dug. This, of course, caused a pother. How to overcome it and get the foundations dry? My father solved it! 'Why not direct the stream through the building and make a big swimming pool in the basement?' This was done. As we all know, the R.A.C. swimming pool is still one of the best in London.

After 1918 Mr. Prüger returned to his native town of Pressburg, a few miles from Vienna. What had been Hungarian was now Czech, and Pressburg had the distinction of three names—Pressburg, Pozony, and Bratislava. Mr. Prüger, however, made the best of it and almost rebuilt his family's Savoy-Carlton Hotel. Unfortunately, he died shortly afterwards, but two of his sons run very successful hotels in the English West Country today.

Other names that come to mind are Kroell, the first Manager of the new Ritz Hotel, who for many years later ran the Ambassador Hotel in New York; Kerpin, for years General Manager of the Hyde Park Hotel; Russell-Cotes of the Royal Bath Hotel, Bournemouth, and Julian Gelardi—brother of Gustave—who at different times was General Manager of the Savoy, Claridges and the Carlton hotels in London and the Waldorf-Astoria Towers in New York. I mention these, as they may be remembered by the older readers of this book.

After 1926 my father, having seen the new Goring Hotel wing opened and myself settled in, spent more and more time in Europe. He became one of the leaders of the International Hotel Managers' Association and attended all of their meetings in various cities of the world.

When he had no excuses for these trips, he took my mother on 'cures' to Weisser Hirsch above Dresden, to Carlsbad and elsewhere. Weisser Hirsch became his favourite, for his mother was still alive and really quite active for an old lady of ninety-five. The entry to Weisser Hirsch is a narrow street leading up by tram or bus from Dresden, about four miles away.

My grandmother used to take a furnished apartment, with a large sitting-room balcony overlooking the entrance to this street, 'so that she could see all that was going on'. We used to call her 'the hotel porter of Weisser Hirsch'. I do not think my grandmother and my father ever got on well together—and, in fact, this may have been one of his reasons for seeking his career in England. He used to visit her more often in her declining years, however, and only envied her one thing, for, like her, he wished to live to be 100 years old. She died at ninety-nine during the 1939-45 War, and he died—after a stroke which made him bedridden for three years—in 1948, aged seventy-nine.

CHAPTER ONE

Early Days, 1910-19

THE Goring Hotel was opened in March 1910. Even in those days it set a standard of comfort equal to the normal standard of comforts expected today. It was probably the last first-class hotel building to be constructed in London before the 1914-18 War, and set an example in planning and layout which was not copied until well into the 1924-25 era.

In fact, it is only of recent years that standard hotel bedrooms for both single and double occupancy, built to a common plan, have become recognized standards for hotel construction.

The Goring Hotel was not built for a luxury clientele.

Good management and altered conditions over the last decade have helped to make it the first-class hotel it is today.

The hotel was built in Ebury Street with the consent of the Grosvenor Estate (Duke of Westminster), and was financed through a Colonel Trollope of Trollope and Colls, Ltd., the well-known firm of builders.

The lease had fallen in on the property and the whole of that part of Ebury Street and Eaton Lane was a site for slum-clearance. There were upwards of sixty small houses on the site now occupied by our garden, and in fact the murderer of the actor Terry in the Strand in 1906 had been captured in one of them.

The existing Goring Hotel gardens are raised above the adjoining street level only because the demolished houses were left 'on site', the brick rubble covered with turf, and a fountain put in the middle. The old Ebury Street frontage consisted of small Nash-type houses built in 1832, at the same time as Victoria Square.

Here again my father was lucky, for a very serious building recession ('slump' in those days) about 1908-10 made semi-speculative construction of the type of the Goring Hotel quite worthwhile financially if you backed the right man as operative proprietor. And my father had a flair for the hotel business.

Victoria Station was only partly built at that time, and I remember the pile-drivers busy filling in the Chelsea end of Buckingham Palace Road to arrest the marshland and make the ground strong enough to carry heavy trains and platforms.

Both the Spanish Embassy and the American Embassy were in Grosvenor Gardens, the latter consisting of one house of about twenty-five rooms. By 1914 an adjacent house had been acquired to make that Embassy thirty-five rooms. All the other houses were private residences.

*

I was a schoolboy at the time, but I have not forgotten the various aspects of life in those days.

The first thing I remember was a bad crane accident while the hotel was being built. Naturally, cranes then were not what they are now. All scaffolding was a series of poles erected piece by piece and bound into position with rope. A slipped knot was therefore not a very unusual occurrence.

Those were still the days of the horse-drawn buses, with their open top-decks. These buses appeared to run to no particular time-table that made sense. They just got you to your destination. There were the 'Whites', the 'Royal Blues', the 'General', the 'Vanguard', and other private firms, the names of which I forget. They all had the real Cockney bus-driver—a race which has died out today—perched on a sort of platform in front at semi-top-deck level, arrayed in a heavy double-breasted overcoat and wrapped in a large waterproof rug. A long whip and a top hat completed this equipment.

One used to take a top front seat (weather permitting) just to hear Cockney comments bandied with all and sundry. Inside in winter straw was placed on the floor to keep one's feet warm.

Fares were one price only. Extra drag-horses were available
at every slight incline, including Knightsbridge to Hyde Park
Corner, and Hyde Park Corner to the Ritz Hotel—considered
quite steep gradients for horses at the beginning of the century.

Pirate buses abounded, and often took the cream of the
custom from the ordinary buses. A pirate bus would lay in
wait at a bus stop, and dash in front of a regular bus as it came
in sight. It would fill up with the short-fare public and get
away just ahead of the regular service. These pirates had no fixed
routes or time-tables. Hence the term 'pirate'.

Many of the Cockney remarks from driver to driver originated
with this uncontrolled system of transport.

I must admit that on a sunny day one could spend a pleasant
afternoon on top of a bus. My mother often used to take me
for a bus ride to the terminus and back for the sake of the
outing. Drawn by two horses—and three when dragging up
hills—these buses would be considered very small by modern
standards. Inside passengers sat face to face along each side;
on top they faced the horses, as one does today in a motor-bus.

Another thing I remember is the straw which was laid right
across the road to deaden the sound of horses' hoofs in front of
houses in which there was illness. Horses seemed to make a lot
of noise on the wood blocks and stone setts (cobbles) of those
days.

*

Growlers and hansom cabs were the means of transport
for the well-to-do, and had not then been displaced by the
taxi-cab.

The growler was a four-wheeled cab, built somewhat on
the lines of a modern cab, but drawn by a horse, with seats
for four people inside and luggage on top.

The taxi-meter had not been invented, so that one had to
know one's London to know the right fare to pay. These
cab-drivers were past masters at the art of assessment and could
tell to within 6d. what a 'fare' was prepared to pay. Actually,
they had a fixed scale at so much per mile, but who could
assess a mile in the twists and turns of the streets? Then there
was 'waiting time'. Cabbies were always pleased to tell you
how expensive it was to stable and fodder the horse, in what

a good condition he kept his beast, how he polished the harness, etc. And let us admit that some of these cabs were very well turned out, and capable of long distances.

However, the cabbie's earning power was controlled by the capabilities of his horse, so that it was in his best interest to keep his steed in good fettle—apart from the higher fares and Cockney talk, for, unlike a modern taxi, which can roam the streets for twenty-four hours at a time, horses need rest. The water-trough is a thing we miss in our streets today. These massive, oblong granite basins—supplied by the Metropolitan Drinking Trough Association—have mostly vanished.

Near us today one still remains at Hyde Park Corner, and another at the corner of Park Lane and Hamilton Place. Even watering horses had its hazards for the cabby. In winter these troughs frequently froze over, so that after a long fare the horse had to be allowed time to cool off before imbibing quantities of ice-cold water to assuage its thirst.

For fast travel one took a sporting two-seater hansom cab, drawn by a spanking horse. This vehicle, with its high wheels, had the driver perched above the cab on a platform seat behind, overlooking the cab, and controlling his horse by long reins and a long whip. He addressed his passengers through a trap-door in the roof. To keep the 'fare' dry (and to prevent his falling out) a pair of heavy hinged coachwork doors opening outwards were provided, which, when shut, afforded comfort and freedom from draughts. What sights and secrets these hansom cab drivers must have seen when looking down through the trap-door at a couple going home late at night! The name came from a Mr. Hansom who put these two-seater cabs on the road. One trouble, of course, was that when one of the two wheels came off—a not infrequent occurrence—the fall was a long and hard one. Naturally, many horses fell between the shafts on all sorts of vehicles on the slippery roads in winter. One expected to see several such mishaps daily, and took no notice. Today, if one of our few remaining dray-horses falls, a crowd of over-sympathetic people gathers to watch the event and give advice.

The open *fiacre*, as still seen in Vienna, Madrid, and occasionally in Paris, never caught on in London to the same extent as the growler and the hansom cab.

My grandfather on my mother's side was an ivory-turner, a

very lucrative business at the turn of the century. He had a shop
in Bond Street and a home in Sidcup at ten miles' distance (now
within the London Postal District). Every morning and evening
he drove a smart 'phantom' with a fettled horse to business and
back. He was always dressed in double-breasted coat, with a
flower in his buttonhole and carrying an ivory-handled whip
suitably carved. The trappings of his horse were also partly made
of ivory. This was most likely a form of publicity. What we must
realize is that his horse had to be stabled, fed, and watered at
each end of the journey each day. This called for considerable
stabling facilities, not only for the one individual, but for the
thousands of men like him in similar circumstances.

Thus we find that central London had as much ground space
devoted to stabling or mews, as we call them, as to houses.
This is still true, for stabling for two horses and a coach took
up as much ground space as the foundations of a house. That
is why we have hundreds of roads today in London, with mews
backing on to the houses and with cobbled ways for access for
carriages. This, which we Londoners take to be a common sight
in our part of Westminster and Belgravia, must appear very old-
fashioned to overseas visitors, for a stable for horse and coach
took up the space of at least three cars today.

Most of these stable houses—or coachman's quarters—are
used as garages now, or have been converted into small four-
or five-roomed houses which are very picturesque and command
considerable rents.

The pendulum has surely swung. In those days means of
transport and the upkeep and care of horses were considered
No. 1 priority in a household. Now no human obligation is felt
for the cars which are left anywhere in the streets day and night.

The London Underground system—that part of it which
is now known as the Metropolitan and Inner Circle Line—was
in existence early in the century. In fact, it was soon after 1900
that South Kensington started to be used as an hotel centre
because of the faster means of transport from Central London
then coming into use. Faster—but very, very dirty. Trains ran
through the selfsame tunnels that are in use today, but the trains
were steam trains, drawn by small engines belching black smoke.
For mile after mile these tunnels ran underground, and the steam
trains ran through them—just ordinary ten-seat-per-compartment

coaches, foul with smoke and soot. Gloves were essential, for the brass door handles were black with greasy soot. Eyes smarted and mouths became dry with the acrid, inevitable pollution of heavy coal smoke. Underground users changed collars, shirts and cuffs twice a day.

*

Business prospered from the very first at the Goring Hotel, and although a private bathroom leading out of a bedroom was almost unknown, the hotel was nearly always full. This was not so difficult with only fifty rooms to let. The terms of 7s. 6d. per single room with private bathroom and 12s. 6d. per double room with private bathroom were attractive.

The front hall in those days was little more than a passage from the front entrance to the lift—an old hydraulic contraption which was the worry of my father's life. It was too easy to work by just pulling a rope. There was no floor-setter device, and visitors using the lift on their own caused no end of anxiety getting the wretched thing to stop at the right place. Anybody could open the lift gates at any floor—and leave them open—or the lift could start a slow upward or downward movement according to its mood.

The present main lounge was then the dining-room, with the kitchen beneath it, but business was so brisk that within two years the outer (glass) lounge overlooking the garden had to be added to accommodate guests wishing to take a meal.

Our food standard was high.

The hall porter had a small desk at the entrance, and where the enquiry and reception offices now stand was a billiard-room, which nobody seemed to use. That was the fashion of the day: a billiard-room was essential.

The telephone exchange (one of the first of its kind) was placed in what is now the middle of the front hall. Telephones to each bedroom were unknown, the system being to install a 'house telephone' in every room, with one external instrument to each floor. The visitor thus had to be called by house 'phone' and go out of his bedroom to answer the external 'phone' in the corridor.

CHAPTER TWO

Between Wars

4th August, 1914. *War*

Two outstanding memories remain. English hotels in those days had a considerable number of foreign employees—especially in London—over in this country to 'learn the language'. When war was declared, I had the unforgettable recollection of seeing our French and German waiters and cooks going arm-in-arm to Victoria Station on 6th August for embarkation to their home countries, the Germans singing the 'Marseillaise' and the Frenchmen 'Deutschland über Alles'. Little did they realize the bitterness of the fighting ahead and the world upheaval which was then starting.

The other memory was the delivery of bread and milk. One of the first steps on mobilization was the withdrawal of all horses from the streets for active service. Public services thus became immobilized—until on 7th August the old London General Omnibus Company was charged with the task of carrying on bread- and milk-rounds, which had been cut off for three days. By 1914 motor-buses had already partially taken the place of horse-buses, but horses were still considered the more reliable means of transport. Not before or since in London have motor-buses been used for such a task.

Churns of milk (no bottles in those days) were placed on the motor-bus floors, surrounded by unwrapped (no paper either then for that purpose) loaves on the seats in complete disorder, and delivered to the public more or less on cash on demand. Milk was served out of half-pint and pint pewter measures into the customers' own jugs.

1915-19

Those first few months of war, as we all know, caught England quite unprepared, and every sort of makeshift had to be resorted to in order to keep the country going under entirely new conditions.

Naturally, the hotel business suffered, and it was only with an effort that the Goring Hotel kept its doors open.

At the outbreak of war the three large hotels in Northumberland Avenue and Trafalgar Square were commandeered as extra Government offices. These three almost adjacent hotels just behind Whitehall and the War Office—the Grand, the Victoria, and the Metropole—housed thousands of War Office staff in their total capacity of about 1,000 rooms.

Other hotels were similarly commandeered.

When America entered the war it was the turn of the hotels in the Victoria area to be requisitioned. With the American Embassy in Grosvenor Gardens, Belgrave Mansions (now Grosvenor Gardens House), adjacent to the Goring Hotel, was obviously the choice for American headquarters. As the war progressed that accommodation became too restricted, so the Goring Hotel was also taken over.

To make an inventory, remove, store, and account for the complete equipment of an hotel—including the main kitchen range—is an undertaking the magnitude of which the general public cannot be expected to understand.

Every item had to be marked with its room number and entered in a bound inventory, and the entire contents of the establishment had to be removed to a storage warehouse. Even today some of the wardrobes in the older part of the hotel bear the labels put on them in 1916.

So the hotel became the annexe of the big house next-door.

Grosvenor Gardens and the Goring Hotel gardens became 'barrack squares' for troop training, while the offices created in the building were filled with high-grade personnel. We were amused at times by the unaccustomed words of command used by our American friends, such as 'Guns on shoulders *put*', but were dismayed at the wear and tear to our beautiful garden, which soon looked like a barrack square, which in fact it was. . . .

The reason for the removal of our kitchen range soon became apparent, for it was rumoured that a direct-cable communication with the White House in Washington was installed in our kitchen and it became the telephone switchboard room. General Pershing certainly used it very considerably, although I believe his official headquarters remained at the American Embassy in Grosvenor Gardens. In any case, all official communiqués sent by the American Embassy were sent direct from our hotel.

Fortunately for us, the Goring Hotel was nearly the last hotel to be requisitioned. It was also the first to be de-requisitioned as the Americans moved out of England in 1919. We were very lucky in that our war-damage claims were handled direct with the American authorities, who were generous and sympathetic in their settlement. Very little damage or alterations were made during their occupation, and they painted the whole building inside and out as part of general maintenance.

All our furniture came back intact and was replaced in the same positions in the same rooms, which was quite a feat in itself. We were also pressed to take quite a considerable sum for loss of goodwill and for advertising the reopening. My father eventually accepted this, although he knew that advertising was unnecessary, in view of the fact that London was at that time desperately short of hotel bedrooms.

*

The years which followed were years of prosperity.

At that time the Goring Hotel had only four bedroom floors above the ground floor, and in 1922 it was decided to add an additional story on the existing roof. To achieve this object, the elevator had to be raised in height, and to carry the extra weight of the fifth floor steel stanchions had to be erected at each corner of the building and cross-strutted. The extra bedrooms and bathrooms were thus actually 'slung' and constructed from the ceiling downwards. The old existing fourth-floor asphalt roof still remains between the fourth- and fifth-floor levels.

The building of this extra story took place during a period of labour unrest, and there was a definite 'go slow' atmosphere among the building crew. So far behind schedule were the builders that in the end the construction was finished by 'blackleg' labour.

Room rates at that period were 25s. per single room and

bathroom, and 45s. per double bedroom with bathroom; luncheon, 4s. 6d., dinner, 7s. 6d.

Hotel occupancy followed the trend of the times, with a distinct on-season and off-season. December to April was off-season, for the American and tourist traffic did not exist during those months. The middle- and upper-class British—on whom the hotel relied for its existence—went to the South of France at the beginning of the year to enjoy the winter sunshine.

To have more than twenty people staying in the hotel at Christmas or Easter was considered good business.

As soon as Easter was passed, occupancy became better.

May, June, and July were the peak periods, corresponding with the London season. Functions at Buckingham Palace have always been highlights at the Goring, whether it be evening levees (in those days), investitures, garden parties, or presentations. August was generally a very bad month, with most people away on holidays.

1925-39

The year 1925 saw the commencement of a scheme to nearly double the size of the hotel. Adjoining houses up to the corner of Ebury Street and Victoria Square had been acquired some years previously and were let on short tenancies to a dairyman and a wood-floor manufacturer. A Chinese family had the corner shop, while No. 11 Victoria Square was already an annexe to the hotel.

These houses were now all pulled down. Three things came to light during the excavation period.

Firstly, it was found that the Chinese family in the corner house had burrowed down a complete floor and made a cave-like hole in the sand. There were no extra foundations. How they got the sandy sub-soil out I cannot say. However, I have heard that Chinese often do this burrowing in Western cities where a soft sub-soil exists. How true it is I do not know, except that in 1959, during the lining of the sewers, 'strange cellar-like cavities' were found at the spot by the workmen.

The second 'find' was a lucky strike for the firm who undertook the excavation work. They had allowed for the usual London clay sub-strata for Ebury Street from the Thames almost to Grosvenor Gardens. This had in years gone by been marshy ground, liable to swamping by the Thames over centuries when the river ran uncontrolled.

They were delighted, therefore, to find good sharp sand as a subsoil—and profited accordingly by selling it to builders' merchants.

The third 'find' arose out of the second.

We had noted in those days of London winter fogs that the site of the Goring Hotel had always remained fog-free. That is to say, that the area from Grosvenor Gardens to Buckingham Palace Mews always had a light patch of fog only, as compared with a heavy fog-content all around. The find of good dry sand explained this point, for whereas fog clings to clay it fights shy of sand.

London fog up to 1925, in those days of indifferent street lighting and dense coal smoke from every two-story private house, was a serious matter. These fogs used to come up over the Thames Valley when the countryside around London was under frost. The cold air could not rise, and the tens of thousands of London chimneys disgorged smoke from early morning into the mist formed over the river valley, contained by the hills to north and south. Sometimes the fogs would last two or three days, according to the weather, until a wind arose.

So bad were they that I remember walking round Belgrave Square twice looking for the way out to Upper Belgrave Street. I also remember an American offering a taxi-driver £5 to take him 'out in the fog' for five minutes. The taxi-driver refused.

Of course, London has no such fogs today, now that smoke-abatement laws are in force. Most homes and business premises use coke, gas, or electricity for heating and cooking. In fact, on an average Paris has as bad fogs as London, as land-bound aircraft statistics at London and Paris airports will show.

*

Our new building rose to a forfeit time schedule and all seemed well until, early in 1926, the General Strike occurred. The hotel walls were up and the roof was on, the plumbing nearly finished and the bathroom tiling completed. The water supply had been connected. On the evening before the General Strike started, one of the workmen—whether on purpose or by accident—left a tap open at full bore on the fifth floor. This tap ran for three days in the empty building and did a great deal of damage to the ceilings and floors below it before it was found to be flooding the new restaurant and kitchens. It took weeks to dry out, and raised the restaurant parquet floor by about a foot, so that it had to be entirely relaid.

However, all these trials were overcome and the new wing (to the right of the elevator), with its pleasant restaurant and new kitchens beneath, was opened only two months behind schedule in July 1926.

This period, again, was a period of hotel prosperity, with the same seasonal conditions prevailing, until the slump of 1928-9 disorganized the world.

During the slump hotels were hit as badly as any other industry. The public tried to exploit the situation, and even regular visitors were looking for reduced terms. People used to walk from hotel to hotel quoting fictitious low rates offered by rival establishments. That was not so bad, but when clients started saying that they could get accommodation at £1 a day at the Ritz or Grosvenor House, the time had come to call a halt.

A price-pact agreement was made by the bigger London hotels, which had the immediate effect of countering fictitious rate conversations. One only had to say 'I know the rates at *x* Hotel are fixed at a minimum of £*y*' for the bubble to burst.

*

The Victoria area had changed very considerably indeed since the 1919 period. With the expansion of industry, office accommodation became overcrowded in the City of London, and very many of the big firms moved their offices to the West End or Victoria district.

Victoria Street from Westminster Abbey to Victoria Station and on to Grosvenor Gardens became the headquarters of engineering firms, institutes, and associations, a position it still holds today.

Victoria Station had already been established as the Continental traffic centre in place of Charing Cross, and the Airway Terminal was being constructed to take long-distance B.E.A. flights.

This was before the B.O.A.C. took over and reserved the Airway Terminal for inter-Continental and trans-Atlantic flights.

In Grosvenor Gardens itself the fact that all the private houses had gradually been converted into suites of offices tended to change the class of people who frequented the hotel. While the Goring still kept its 'county' connection, more and more leaders of industry visited the establishment because of its proximity to their headquarter offices.

CHAPTER THREE

World War Upsets, 1939-45

1939-45. *War Again*

LOOKING back after fifteen years, the Second World War had its hectic and, as seen through the passing of the years, its amusing incidents.

At the outbreak of hostilities London became a semi-deserted city, for tens of thousands of its inhabitants were evacuated to the country.

On the first day of the declaration of war—in fact, within one hour of the official outbreak of hostilities—a false air raid alarm was sounded, which drove everyone to shelter. I happened to be in Croydon at the time, and went to an air raid shelter near the very big gas-works in that town. Several people in the shelter were discussing the probable effects of a direct hit on these gas-works. Conversation got from just jittery to almost hysterical, until a middle-aged man, obviously employed at the gas-works, joined in with a casual remark: 'I reckon that if a bomb went right through one of our gas-containers, it would be so surprised at the amount of gas inside that it would forget to go off.' A clever remark aptly said at the right moment. The 'All Clear' sounded a minute later.

During the few months before the declaration of war many of us had been taking air raid precaution (A.R.P.) instruction. Apart from dealing with incendiary bombs, we were instructed in methods of combating poison-gas bombs.

This instruction really made us think, for we were told that Lewisite gas bombs landing in Trafalgar Square would contaminate that square for from thirty-six to forty-eight hours, with positive danger to lungs and lives. In fact, these lectures made us much more scared than the events which followed.

*

The hotel was empty except for six people. To give a better feeling of confidence, we had a movable screen erected in the restaurant, leaving only twelve tables at the top-window end, and dispensing with three-quarters of the main room. As business improved in the following years we moved this wooden-panelled screen back, and in 1942 took it down altogether. An air raid shelter, fitted up with bunks, was made in the basement. The top floor was evacuated and the mattresses, chairs, etc., deployed to this basement shelter. Several of the staff were instructed in emergency first-aid duties.

Many of our younger staff were obviously absorbed in the Armed Forces. Many others volunteered for factory jobs in the early days, and their services were lost to us for some years. It is surprising how many of them came back to us to take up their old jobs after 1945, and shows the good relationship which has always existed at the Goring. We kept the hotel open, but at great financial loss, for the first two years.

*

Our head kitchen chef, a Frenchman, reported at the French Embassy in 1939, and was told to report to his Army head-quarters at Nancy, France. He left his wife and English-born family, and after several days in cattle-trucks in a journey across France he duly reported. On interview he was asked his age, which he gave. Had he a family in England? Yes—wife and two children. His age at that time put him in the highest category for call-up. But, according to French military law, your family puts one year per person on to your age, so that his official age for war purposes was three years past call-up. He was dismissed and spent several weeks and much money in returning to England by devious routes to take up his duties at the Goring Hotel again.

*

Soon after this we had our first and only taste of bombing. About 7 p.m. one evening an unobliging raider dropped a

Molotov breadbasket (incendiary bomb cradle) on the hotel. Incendiaries landed in the roadway, in the hotel garden, in the area in front of the hotel, and on the flat asphalt roof. Two in the area outside the kitchen window, the sector controlled by my chef, recently returned from France, started burning. Those in the road and garden were easily handled. Not, however those outside the kitchen. Chef came to the kitchen door, and did nothing. 'These have fallen on concrete; they will burn out. In any case, I have my chickens in the oven for dinner and have no time for *imbecilites*.' So we put them out ourselves. . . .

It was just then that we got an urgent call from the roof. Several bombs called for immediate attention. This was simple: the trained team just had to use the long-handled shovels lying handy to push them off the roof on either side on to the pavement in front or the garden at the back.

I personally covered a bomb with sand to smother it, as I had been instructed at A.R.P. lectures. This bomb was on the middle of the roof, and all the long-handled shovels were in use at the time. That appeared to be the end of the matter. It had all been so simple. But half an hour later we had another urgent call to the top floor, where an incendiary had burnt through the roof and lodged in an air-duct shaft. This had been seen by roof-watchers on the building opposite, and we were duly warned by telephone. Yes, it was my sweet little incendiary, the one I had so cleverly covered with sand to smother it. I had forgotten for the moment that it had fallen on an asphalt roof and could burn through.

As previously stated, the top floor had been evacuated some months before, and all furniture and carpets removed, in order to give working space for just such an eventuality. All the baths functioned and the water had not been cut off. Fire-fighting with stirrup-pumps fed from the baths was thus not a difficult matter.

Having cut away the air-shaft with axes, we were soon able to handle the outbreak with the stirrup-pumps.

*

A great strain on the staff was caused by the 'black-out' control. Every evening at dusk, throughout the war, the black curtains had to be closed at every window in every room in the hotel. Particularly anxious times, from my point of view, were spring and autumn. In other words, the change from summer to winter and winter to summer. One had got the day staff nicely coached in curtain-drawing during the winter, when the days were shorter, and this came before 8 p.m. In the summer it became the duty of the night staff to take over 'black-out' duties. This invariably caused confusion and forget-fulness for the first few days in either case, and many a time a cry from a patrolling warden in the street to 'Put that —— light out' was heard. Too many 'Put that —— light out' shouts eventually led to a summons.

One night we tripped up badly. It had been snowing quite hard and the ground in the garden was white. On that particular night a burglar decided to visit us—or, rather, to visit a guest in a room two floors above my private suite. He must have climbed a drain-pipe outside my window in a very adept manner to get into the bedroom above, for we heard nothing at all, although we were sitting quietly talking in my sitting-room. Suddenly an irate Army officer burst into my room: 'I've been robbed.'

We hurried to his bedroom, and sure enough his room had been ransacked. Nothing appeared to have been taken, however, except a box of chocolates which the officer had brought with him from Cairo that day—presumably for his wife or family. After a search next day, we found the box of chocolates, nearly empty, in the garden under a hedge outside my window. It seemed peculiar, but nothing more was said at the time.

What did transpire, however, was the fact that in our excite-ment and subsequent search we had left the curtains wide open in the officer's room, and the light was shining with more than usual intensity on the snow. . . .

Police Court next morning. Fine, £5.

This story had a sequel. In 1957 I was visiting Spain, when a man staying at the same hotel came up to me and asked if I had anything to do with the Goring Hotel.

I replied in the affirmative. He then introduced himself as the person who had been robbed during the war.

I asked him how it happened that he had nothing stolen except a box of chocolates. He smiled, and told me that he had been a British agent in those days, and had been sent back to England with urgent private papers.

'Not what you thought—chocolates for my girl friend. Fortunately, I had the papers in my body-belt. My opposite number thought I might have hidden them in the chocolates.'

*

After 1942 London became much more frequented and life got back to near normal, although food-rationing was a considerable trial. All sorts of people, mostly in uniform, frequented the hotel. On one occasion a British naval officer arrived from the Far East and went straight to the Admiralty late at night to report. During his absence from the hotel the chambermaid went to tidy his room in the ordinary course of her duties. She came screaming down the corridor. 'There's an enormous rat in his bed,' she yelled. Being unused to such things, we at once investigated. We found a very friendly tame mongoose. However, we had to ask him to leave the hotel, as he would not be parted from his pet; which brought a reprimand from the Admiralty. Our viewpoint was that we cannot afford to have tame mongooses in the hotel; the ladies do not like them.

On another occasion two Russian Generals occupied a double bedroom. They had a very large tin of caviar, which they refused to have deposited in the cold-room (possibly with reason in those days). They preferred to keep it in their bedroom cupboard. That cupboard smelt for months afterwards, for the oil had leaked out and penetrated the woodwork.

At one period twenty young American naval officers arrived at the hotel. They were assigned to the Archangel Patrol and were passing through London to join their vessel. Each one had an immense Service chest containing fleece coats, etc., for cold weather in the Arctic. These chests looked just like coffins, and they wanted them all up in their bedrooms, even for the one night of their visit. Staff were not too plentiful in those days, so they were asked to leave their luggage in our store, as they were all locked and labelled. It was also explained to them that it might look bad for the hotel if twenty coffin-like objects left the hotel floors at one time. . . . They saw the point. . . .

*

Fire-watching continued throughout the war. We were divided into sections and expected to take up 'look-out' positions on different roofs in order to report the fall of any bombs. Thus we all got to know each other from roof to roof and would carry on long conversations. As the war progressed, however, fire-watching took on a different aspect.

It was my custom to be on the roof for every night raid, and from 1942 onwards I was generally accompanied by American Service personnel who wanted to 'see the fun'. Many of these officers had never been under fire and would stand on the roof watching the shell-bursts most enthusiastically. Many were the occasions when I had to shout, after certain shell-bursts, 'Get down under that chimney breast.' 'Why?' they asked. 'Never mind. You'll see. Take cover,' I'd reply. Sure enough, within a short time a handful of shell splinters would land on the roof. In many ways this was an embarrassment, as if anyone had been hit I might have been blamed for letting them 'see the fun'.

We are so near to Buckingham Palace that the land-mine which hit our Royal Residence one night moved all the beds in the section of the hotel facing the Palace—not only moved them, but swung them from one end of the room over to the window end.

A bomb fell very near us one night and hit a bank in Grosvenor Gardens. I was the first on the scene, just in time to stop a taxi falling into the crater formed, which was hidden by the rising dust. A water main burst and flooded the bank strong-room. The next day certain nearby establishments had £10,000 in £5 banknotes being dried on clothes-lines in their boiler-houses. . . .

On that well-remembered fatal Sunday when a bomb hit the Guards' Chapel during Matins, three of our guests failed to return. Being delayed, the then Colonel of the Regiment arrived late. He did not like to go in and make himself conspicuous—and so his life was saved. . . .

One day our Head Waiter did not appear for the evening meal. I had been sitting in a train in Victoria Station for some time, as the train was held up owing to an air raid then in progress. I heard a couple of V2's fall not far away. Eventually the train started on its journey. Our Head Waiter was never seen again.

Such were the hazards of those times. Men and women
follow different mental processes where bombing is concerned.
Men did not seem to like bombing by aeroplane with the
drone and expectation of a hit as the planes got nearer. V1s
and V2s did not worry them at all.

My wife used to sleep through all the air raids in the earlier
days of the war. We never went to an air raid shelter, nor did
we put our very young children in shelters, for the sudden
cold and damp of underground quarters in the cold of night
might have affected their health—or at least have given them
continuous colds and affected them more than the chance of
a direct hit.

But V1s and V2s were different. Women seemed to have
an uncontrollable fear of sudden death without the warning
drone of aeroplanes overhead.

I discussed this point with hundreds of people of both sexes
during the war and am convinced of the fundamental difference
in mentality between the two sexes on this question.

*

The war over, everyone hoped that things would right
themselves quickly. This was not to be, however, for food
controls, building controls, furniture controls, fuel controls,
wine controls, whisky controls, and other controls galore
continued to hinder and embarrass us until well into 1950. The
fuel controls only came off in 1958.

All those hotels which had weathered the storm, however,
enjoyed great prosperity.

A bed was a bed, and they were sold as such. Many a time
two people—so long as they were of the same sex—were told
to share a twin-bedded room, rather than have an empty bed.
The alternative was to sleep on the Embankment. This congestion gradually put itself right as things got back to normal,
but overcrowding conditions continued until well into 1950.

The great change at the Goring has been its increase in
restaurant service. Pre-war, if we did forty-five luncheons and
sixty dinners we had had a good day.

Since the war, however, the meals served, especially lunches,
have risen 300 per cent. This has continued right up to the
present day and, although four small private dining-rooms and

an expensive self-service room of cold dishes have been added, the space is still not enough.

This great restaurant activity is bound up in the yet greater expansion of office accommodation up Grosvenor Place to Hyde Park Corner, following expansion from Victoria Street and Grosvenor Gardens. The Goring is certainly the nearest first-class establishment to attract the many important heads of industry in this vast office area, containing, as it does, the headquarter buildings of so many private and national industries in England.

To try to obtain greater elasticity, various houses have been bought up near the hotel, with a view to solving a staff housing problem and to create more working space within the hotel itself. Many improvements have been made inside the building: bathrooms have been remodelled and some of the older rooms equipped with built-in furniture specially made to be in keeping with our mildly 'Georgian' architecture. Built-in furniture gives extra floor space without lessening cupboard room.

CHAPTER FOUR

Our Garden

OUR little garden has always been a well-kept oasis at the back of the hotel. An oasis which contains water, green grass, shrubs, and flowers.

As mentioned elsewhere in this book, the Goring Hotel was built on a slum-clearance site. To perpetuate our 'open space', a three-party agreement was entered into between the Grosvenor Estate, the Westminster City Council, and ourselves. We undertook the upkeep of the garden and, provided we did not charge an 'upkeep' payment from the surrounding houses, we could keep the garden private. This has been strictly adhered to, for we would rather maintain it ourselves than have other people exercising dogs, sitting in deck-chairs, or leaving rubbish about.

Before the slum clearance in 1908, tenement houses backed on to the existing houses in Victoria Square, and narrow, unlit passages ran at right angles from Eaton Lane. Once these houses were pulled down and the garden made, the tenants in Victoria Square commenced to open out their party wall in order to obtain a view of the garden and to get more light into their big back rooms.

The laws governing the occupation of land, freehold and leasehold rights, are very complicated in England.

The Goring Hotel and gardens were leased by the Grosvenor Estate for a term of ninety-nine years at an agreed rental. Actually no rental was payable on the gardens, the assessment being on the hotel. Central London freehold is, of course, very valuable— especially an island site. So when the Grosvenor Estate sold the freehold of a large site (containing the Metropole Cinema,

Moyses Stevens, the florist, etc.) in Victoria Street, we thought we might try for our own freehold. After a lot of negotiation with various people in the Grosvenor Estate office, someone at last persuaded the Duke of Westminster to surrender the lease and grant us our freehold.

There was the usual conveyance map attached to the deed. On it was marked in red a narrow strip of land, 6 feet in width, running the whole length of the garden up against the houses in Victoria Square and approximately the size of our existing bed of shrubs. The Grosvenor Estate reserved itself the right to use this strip of land to add depth to the Victoria Square houses, should the time ever come for rebuilding.

At the moment this is most unlikely, as Victoria Square is marked on the town-planning maps as being of historical and architectural value, and it cannot therefore be altered.

The Grosvenor Estate charges us a rental of 1s. per annum for the use of this strip of land until such time as they claim it.

This rental is paid twice yearly in the sum of 6d. At the time of writing this book, to collect 6d. the Estate has to post a letter (3d.) and use an expensively printed demand form and an envelope. We, on our side, have to write a cheque costing 2d. and return the bill for 3d. postage. The Estate then has to return our receipt for 2d. postage. The total cost, therefore, to receive 6d. is 10d., without overhead expenses and salaries—and this twice a year!

Our garden, besides having received incendiary bombs, receives and welcomes all sorts of birds. For twenty years now a blackbird and its offspring have nested in the ivy-covered wall. Its song early on a spring or summer morning is so refreshing, and is the delight of our many country visitors.

As well as being one of the best shots in Europe, King George V, during his reign, kept a variety of birds in a sanctuary in the grounds of Buckingham Palace—fancy birds he had brought down from Sandringham and Balmoral. On many occasions in those days golden pheasants used to adorn our garden—in between the times their wings were clipped by Buckingham Palace staff.

At all times ornamental water birds from St. James's Park frequent our little fountain pond. One day last year one flew into the garden and immediately laid an egg on the paving surrounding the pool. It returned, with its drake, for many days afterwards looking for its egg, which had rolled into the pond. This year (1960) a duck with two drakes made their home in the garden. She hatched 9 ducklings on the top of the tool-shed, 7 feet high, and brought them down one at a time on her back to the pond. They were quite a talking-point for weeks!

Naturally, every visitor wants a bedroom overlooking the garden. Unfortunately, only one-third of our rooms face this aspect. Our response to these requests is that the rooms overlooking the front are quieter than those overlooking the garden. Ebury Street and Victoria Square are extremely quiet after 11.30 p.m. Not so the garden side—it depends on the number of stray cats about at the time! I think the only reason the duck reared her chicks was because all the stray cats vanished in 1959 for some unknown reason.

We have always been lucky with our gardeners at the Goring Hotel. From the commencement and for many years afterwards we had the Head Gardener of the Archbishop of Canterbury at Lambeth Palace.

When he retired, about 1928, I was hard put to find a replacement. I hit on the happy idea of strolling into St. James's Park close by, approaching a gang of about twenty men laying out a flower-bed, and asking for the foreman. A man stood forward, obviously thinking I came from the Office of Works, which controls the Royal Parks. I explained what I wanted. He thought he might be able to find someone suitable. Could he think it over? Of course, he came himself the same evening. For about thirty years now this system has run very smoothly. As each man retires from the Park foremanship he delegates his successor. The first holder of the position delegated this post to Jack Hobbs, who always made the remark, 'I'm Jack Hobbs, but I don't play cricket.'

He was followed by an excellent gardener named Cook. Cook was Head Gardener at Marlborough House, the home of the late Queen Mary. He not only did the gardening, but also arranged the personal flowers for her reception-rooms and her bedroom. So well was he thought of that he had the honour of taking his turn to mount guard at her lying-in-state.

When Queen Mary died, I regretfully lost the services of Mr. Cook. He did not retire; on the contrary, he was promoted foreman at Hampton Court Palace, with twenty-eight gardeners under him. Before leaving, he handed over our little garden to the excellent man who still presides over it.

To avoid any misunderstanding with any possible powers that be, let me make it quite plain that our garden is by no means a full-time job. The garden is maintained entirely out of normal working hours—after 6 p.m. in the summer and for about one to two hours on a Saturday in the winter, before it gets dark. One of the troubles is the grass, which may look all right from the hotel windows, but is in reality most patchy and the lawn very uneven, despite all kinds of lawn-dressing, for it is actually grown on brick rubble deposited there in 1908.

*

I can safely say that we are known for our flower-boxes of geraniums in the summer. Long before the war they were a feature of the hotel, and in those days were maintained by Moyses Stevens, the well-known florist.

Since the war, however, I acquired a country house with quite a spacious garden, and have been able to take my own cuttings and bring them on under glass.

My original stock of Gustav Emmich geraniums has a history. For the Peace Parade in 1945-6 the flower-beds around the Queen Victoria Memorial outside Buckingham Palace were specially planted with these geraniums. For three days the crowds milled about these beds and bruised the plants so badly as to completely spoil their chance of survival. They were all taken up as useless—except for about 600 cuttings which I obtained from my gardener. My same stock still survives today.

In 1939 I planted a vine against a wall in the garden. The weather that year was very kind to us. The vine produced forty-three bunches of grapes. Since then it has not borne fruit. I did not realize then that outdoor vines need very drastic pruning each year. It is still ornamental—but not useful.

*

During the last war, owing to prevailing circumstances, we had to make our flower-beds and some sections of the border into a vegetable garden. One can make a most attractive flower-bed if one sows with tomatoes, red cabbage, curly kale, dwarf spinach, and a garden herb border. This looks very nice until picking/ cutting time, which, naturally, upsets the formation.

One year during the war we got nearly 200 lb. of outdoor tomatoes from the hotel garden, which shows what a sun-trap— free from winds—our garden is.

CHAPTER FIVE

Anecdotes and Reminiscences

A DIPLOMAT of a certain age, who shall remain nameless, decided to remarry into a very influential English family. He took a whole floor at the Goring Hotel and put himself and his eight children on one side of the corridor and his wife-to-be with her six children on the other side of the corridor. This continued for two weeks before the ceremony. All the 'children' were seventeen years of age or more. A diplomatic diplomat!

*

Like all hotels, we have our 'jungle telephone'. Whenever Mr. Perrin walked into the hotel at lunch-time the restaurant was at once flashed a message, 'Worcester Sauce'.

Lady Palmer, however, was not so easy to please. In those days I used to supply Carr's cheese assorted biscuits in quarter-tins with the cheese course. These tins, containing several kinds of cheese biscuits, were most attractively packed with white corrugated paper surrounding the different varieties. By a trick in packing, these surrounding papers never became disarranged until nearly all the biscuits had been taken. Also, I preferred the actual baking of the biscuits.

Lady Palmer, however, would have none of this. She tried her very best on many occasions to persuade me to buy from her family firm. She sent a works manager to see me, got out sample tins—in fact, did everything she could. The works never got the packing right, although they tried to copy the rival firm's methods.

Actually, we were the first hotel to use these quarter-tins of assorted cheese biscuits back in 1925. We found the half-tins too wasteful and untidy, for as soon as the top layer had been partly used—or even before—people started diving down to the lower layer and making the box untidy, in order to find the kinds they liked best. These were invariably the sweeter ones. We therefore suggested a quarter-tin to Messrs. Carr & Co., with no bottom layer. This was agreed to at almost the same price, if we would serve the biscuits in the box, as the whole effect lay in the presentation of the assortment. We willingly agreed.

The idea was copied by other hotels.

Today, however, only the half-tins are available. We tried to reintroduce the old quarter-pack after the war—as recently as 1956, but the cost of packing made the actual biscuits 250 per cent. more than buying in half or whole square tins.

Such is 'progress' in an industry which has been rationalized into a type of combine. If you want to see how untidy a half-tin can get, take a meal in a railway dining-car. Do not blame the staff for the untidiness of the tin when it has been round the diners.

Animals

There is a notice in the hall of the Goring Hotel stating:

VISITORS ARE RESPECTFULLY REMINDED THAT DOGS, CATS BIRDS, AND OTHER PETS ARE NOT ALLOWED IN ANY PART OF THIS HOTEL —

This rule has been strictly enforced since 1910.

There are exceptions to every rule, but not many in our case.

The first exception was in 1912. Muffs were still fashionable at that time. A lady brought a marmoset in her muff one day and was assigned a room on the first floor, with access to the balcony on the front. Being a warm night, she left the balcony window open. The next morning we had a continuous stream of phone calls from rooms all along the balcony. One room reported that the things on the dressing table had been dis-arranged 'in some unaccountable way'. Another reported that some papers had been tampered with. A lady reported—in a shamed voice—that her toupé had vanished. (We found this later further along the balcony.)

At last a sleepy and irritable male voice explained that *he had* just woken up from a deep sleep, and there was a monkey sitting on his chair. Somehow, he felt sure it was a live one!

A few years later—muffs still being worn—a certain regular guest with whom we were very friendly in the hotel came down one morning and produced a baby Pekinese out of her muff. We had a good laugh about it, but I have reason to believe the story went the rounds of Mayfair!

Two young American women were found with an Airedale in their bedroom one afternoon after their arrival.

I was informed and went up to see them.

They used the wrong approach with: 'Mr. Manager, all rules are made to be broken. Here's a £5 note.'

A member of the staff was at once sent to pack their luggage and they departed.

The reverse was an experience I had with a very well-known and influential visitor from the country. He was of a fiery dis-position and used to making his own decisions. On one visit he arrived for the night with a fine red setter, and it was obvious that he was passing through London after a week-end shooting with friends.

I spoke to him in the hall and was called all sorts of things: 'Who was I to interfere with the liberty of the subject. . . . His dog, he would do what he liked with,' etc. When he had calmed down a little, I just asked him:

'Well, sir, where do you keep this truly beautiful setter at home?'

'Why, in the k . . .' He looked at me. 'Oh, all right. You win,' and we shook hands on it. We were friendly for years afterwards.

About 1930 wire-haired terriers were all the rage. A very charming American family had been staying at the Goring for about a fortnight. On the day of their departure for home, the husband came to me and told me he had paid a very high price for a pedigree wire-haired terrier dog, from which he wished to breed in America. The dog had been kennelled at Harrods for the past week. He knew the hotel rules, but, as he was leaving in a few hours for his boat train, could he have the dog in the hotel? I said, 'No,' but I would take care of the animal for him.

He was a fine, high-spirited dog, so I put him over in the garage, tied to a stout length of sash-cord, and properly supplied with food and drink. All very simple—until someone dashed across from the garage to say that the dog had bitten through its leash and had escaped.

I was left with exactly one hour to find him in the streets of London! Where to start looking—north, south, east, or west? Obviously a job for the police. I dare not ask the owner for a full description and had to give a rough description from memory. 'Was there a collar round his neck?' 'Yes, because he was tied to a wall by a piece of sash-cord which he had bitten through.'

That last remark saved me. Half an hour later a policeman arrived leading the dog. It had been picked up trying to enter Buckingham Palace!

My terrible visions of compensation, of exporting the dog to the United States, the anger of the owner, and other unpleasant possibilities vanished. I handed over the animal to its owner with a smile half an hour later. Only the dog and I know of his glorious half-hour's freedom in the London streets.

*

Many early guests to the Goring Hotel still visit us regularly. For instance, Mr. Alexander Watson was amongst our first regular clientele. Only recently in 1959 he told me of his enthusiasm for the hotel.

His story is that he first came to the Goring in November 1910. He was then a young man on a week-end visit from the University and was accompanied by three Varsity friends,

Ashley Player, John Lauder, and Stuart Truell—all in Town to attend a Law Society dinner.

On the train down to London, Mr. Watson mentioned to his friends that a 'smashing' new hotel, with a bathroom to every bedroom, had recently been opened, and suggested they should stay there.

Ashley Player (son of the Player family of tobacco fame) asked, 'Is it expensive, because I haven't got much money?' John Lauder (son of Harry Lauder—later Sir Harry) did not think he could afford the cost. Stuart Truell thought it might be expensive. The actual cost was, as I have reported in another chapter, 7s. 6d. per single bedroom with private bathroom.

*

It is not often the name of the Goring Hotel has appeared in the Divorce Courts. One occasion well before the First World War is worth recording, however.

We had a martinet of an Irish Catholic Head Receptionist at that time, named Miss Jarvis. Naturally, Miss Jarvis did not hold with divorce. However, she was subpoenaed, so she had to attend at the Law Courts to give evidence of occupancy of a hotel bedroom. She found herself confronted by a stern judge we all knew.

He asked her the usual questions: 'Was the room mentioned in this case a double room? Had room No. 57 got two beds or one double bed?'

Miss Jarvis got annoyed at these silly questions. She replied: 'You ought to know, my Lord. You have slept there often enough!'

*

Just before the Second World War we had a very charming old lady of about eighty living in the hotel. As time went on, however, her health began to deteriorate. During the last few months of her stay she would come down before lunch and call for a double liqueur brandy. Having had her brandy, she would go to the restaurant entrance, chart a straight line to her corner table at the other side of the room, and walk straight ahead. She never missed her table, and I do not think many people noticed her intense expression of concentration as she crossed the room.

However, when she started removing her teeth and washing

them in her water goblet between courses, I thought the time had come to take action. It is very difficult for a much younger man to tackle a grandmother on a question of this kind. I thought out what I considered to be a good escapist exercise.

She had a son in Holy Orders. Here was the man for the job— his own mother, too! He had to listen to my suggestions that he spoke to his mother, but no one ever gave me a dirtier look!

Unfortunately the old lady began to fail seriously shortly afterwards and left the hotel.

*

A hotel manager's life is very varied, and he must be prepared for almost anything at short notice without showing a sign as to his inner feelings.

One Saturday afternoon I was supervising a very lively wedding reception when a guest asked to speak to me. I knew the lady—a Canadian—had lost her husband two days previously in a nursing-home, as he had been taken ill at the Goring. She proceeded to ask me for information as to the means of shipping a corpse to Canada, the cost of a lead-lined coffin—would it remain airtight, and how long would it take to make?

*

It is surprising how many guests lose things and come to the hotel office and say they have been robbed.

While robberies will happen, unfortunately, in even the best run hotels, they are actually few and far between.

By and large an hotel bedroom is much more difficult to rob than a country house. A would-be thief must first of all have a key to the self-closing lock of a guest's bedroom, and he must also be fairly certain of what is behind the guest's door. The guest may be in his bedroom, or in the bathroom; in which case the would-be thief can only say, 'I'm sorry, I've got the wrong number.' Then, a member of the staff may see a stranger trying to enter the wrong bedroom. This is a haphazard way of setting about a burglary and must be nerve-racking for the burglar.

An 'inside job' is also not so easy as one might think, for we know our staff, where they should be at a given time and those who have pass keys. Suspicion, therefore, generally falls on new-comers and the suspicions are usually correct.

However, sometimes genuine mistakes are made. Take the

case of the man who came to see me one morning and reported that his pocket-book had been stolen. 'It must have been taken by the floor waiter who served my breakfast!' he said. He wanted the floor waiter and his pantry searched. I accompanied him to his bedroom, and the first thing I saw was his pocket-book wedged by the bedlight to keep the shade in the particular position he wished it to be.

On another occasion two ladies came to my office. They had been robbed of a roll of $500 bills. One lady haltingly confided to me that she always kept this roll of $500 securely fastened to her suspender at the top of her stocking, so that it could not possibly have been lost. A few hours later I received a telephone call from the Police Lost Property Department. 'I've got a taxi-driver here. Says he found a wad of dollar notes in his taxi yesterday afternoon. The fare was picked up at your hotel. Do you know anything about it?'

One day a 'confidence man' used the gentlemen's cloakroom to see what he could find. An obviously well-to-do American walked in, took off his coat, hung it up on a peg, and proceeded to wash his hands. The confidence man went into action—'I say, Sir, you've got some filthy mess on your coat. I'll wipe it off for you while you wash.' 'Thanks' said the American and continued his ablutions. The American put on his coat and left the cloakroom. Ten minutes later he came to me and said he had been robbed of $2,000 in travellers' cheques, passport, and about £5 in cash. I sent for the Police, who took particulars. The next morning I received a parcel containing passport, $2,000 (unsigned) travellers' cheques, and a pocket-book. The Police came and proudly handed over the returned goods, and thus made a very good impression with our American visitor. The sequence to this anecdote was that our American guest—being a High Court Judge in the United States—was given two seats for the Trooping of the Colour, with the compliments of the Commissioner of Police (London) as an apology for the inconvenience which he had been caused.

*

In good hotel kitchens the orders are given in French. This implies that waiters have a reasonable knowledge of that language, and as many of them at the Goring are European-trained waiters, in London to learn English on the exchange system, this is not normally difficult.

On one occasion, however, a young English lad from Lancashire, who was shaping into quite a good waiter, was told by the head waiter to get some *pommes pailles* (straw potatoes). He went to the kitchen and asked for a 'plum pie'. He was duly cursed by the Chef, and told it would take an hour to make. Fortunately, he reported this to the head waiter who had time to correct the misunderstanding.

*

As a young man, I remember making the same type of mistake. I was working as a waiter in French Switzerland at the time and was asked by a customer for some *cure-dents* (tooth-picks). I had never heard the word before, so I went to the kitchen and shouted my order in the approved style I was accused of being cheeky and had a frying-pan flung at me for my trouble.

*

Right at the beginning of the war in 1939 a certain Air Vice-Marshal, and a particular friend of the family, flew over the Sahara. He spotted a particularly fine fat deer. He flew in low and shot it. The next day he arrived at the Goring Hotel and proceeded to feast his friends on three separate occasions off this succulent animal. The head is still preserved today.

On the same trip he picked up a species of date lizard. Unthinkingly, he left this lizard in a box with his old mother in a flat nearby and went out with friends to a party. His mother opened the box lid and saw a very shrunken and wrinkled object at the bottom, stretched out as if dead. Thinking it might have been her fault that the lizard had died, and not wanting to upset her noble son, she decided to try to revive it. So, putting a few drops of brandy and water in a saucer in the box, she put the box by the fire and went on with her knitting.

She must have dozed in the hot room, for on awakening she was confronted with an enormous, blown-out lizard many times the size of the one she had tried to revive, and hurriedly shut the box lid, thinking she must have had the brandy, and not the 'dead' reptile!

Only when her son returned and told her that the lizard was

behaving quite naturally under warm conditions was she appeased.

At one time during the war this Air Vice-Marshal was stationed at High Wycombe, and was assigned a particularly dumb batman. Having been brought up (and I believe born) in the Far East, he had some very fine specimens of Chinese art. One valuable vase he was particularly attached to, and always had it on his mantelpiece. One day his batman dropped this precious vase. Now, 'Ronnie' had an appalling temper at times. On this occasion he really went for his batman. After calling him all the names he could think of, he finished up: 'This vase was made 2,000 years B.C. It is therefore nearly 4,000 years old today. It has been handled by thousands of people during these 4,000 years, but it needs a bloody clot of a batman to break it.' Most probably the vase was not as old as he stated, but he certainly made his point!

*

Before the war there was a famous Stock Exchange/financier crisis in Paris of the type which crops up once every generation. It was known as the Stavinsky Case. Stavinsky was declared bankrupt for an enormous sum, with international repercussions.

At the time it was rumoured that Madame Stavinsky had visited England just before the crash and had deposited a very considerable fortune in jewellery in London. It was also rumoured that some of the Russian Imperial jewels were included in this cache.

The case made headlines for months in the world's newspapers, but the jewellery was never found.

One day, shortly before the Coronation of King George VI, a very well-known jeweller from the Rue de la Paix, Paris, and well known at the Goring, arrived at the hotel. Having taken a sitting-room suite, he and his companion went out 'for a walk'. An hour later he returned with some parcels, which he had collected from another well-known jeweller and pawnbroker not very far from the hotel.

He sent for me and asked me to put them in the hotel safe for custody. 'You had better look at them first,' he said, and proceeded to open the jewel-cases.

There lay before me a marvellous collar of long emeralds set with diamonds—each emerald about an inch long—a bracelet to match, and a tiara, brooches, ear-rings, and hundreds of loose pearls and diamonds of varying sizes, from very small to very large.

I at once said I could not be responsible for this marvellous treasure, as our burglar insurance was not heavy enough and our safe was not equipped to withstand the efforts of international safe-breakers. To have been robbed and lose a case for damages would certainly have made the hotel bankrupt.

I suggested therefore that he kept them at his own responsibility and left the jewels hidden in his suite—nobody except the hotel office knew his room number. He refused, and insisted I put them in the safe, as no one could possibly know he was staying at the hotel and the risk was negligible.

I pointed out that, to the contrary, he was a very well-known international jeweller whom any person from a safe-breaking organization could not possibly lose track of, if they wanted him shadowed. (He stood well over 6 feet and carried the scar of an enormous sword-cut from eye to chin.)

So I made out a typewritten document relieving the hotel of responsibility, which he reluctantly signed, and then I put the treasure in the safe.

In every hotel bedroom in England there is a statement to the effect that the management does not hold itself responsible in law for valuables except if deposited in the hotel safe. English law in those days laid down that an innkeeper was not liable for the negligence of a guest in this respect over the sum of £30, in the event of robbery.

To have left the jewellery in the suite of rooms would have relieved me of responsibility, for, in case of robbery, I could have claimed negligence on the part of the owner. He evidently knew this and tried to protect himself. The next morning he took his jewel collection away, and it was rumoured that he had come over specially to try to sell some of the jewels in connection with the approaching Coronation. Whether this last rumour is true or not, I cannot say, but it seems probable.

*

Our daughter was born in the hotel in 1935. She arrived somewhat unexpectedly—so much so that my wife was playing cards with my parents up to 11 p.m. and the baby was born at 2 a.m. I went out to a dinner appointment with the Reunion des Gastronomes (an hotel society of leading managers, of which I was later President).

Before leaving the hotel, I said I would sleep in Room 104—if I was wanted—but told only the nurse of this intention. On my return, after midnight, I found that Room 104 had been let, so I took another room and slept in No. 110.

Soon after 2 a.m. the nurse went to Room 104, knocked at the door and said that a beautiful baby daughter had been born. Imagine the surprise of the nurse and the utter consternation of the Frenchman who opened the door to hear this news. '*Moi— c'est impossible—beaucoup trop vite.*'

This daughter of ours attracted considerable attention during the first few years of her life. She got friendly with a very tall, hard-bitten bachelor who had spent most of his life in Hong Kong and Shanghai.

One morning, when she was three years old, she came bouncing into the hotel, quite full of herself, to meet this gentleman in the middle of the front hall. 'Good morning, Mr. Smith. I am so excited. I was told that if I was good I would have a baby brother to play with. I have been so very, very good that I have two baby brothers to play with. I told Mummy to give them my bedsheet. You see, I don't wet my bed any more now, Mr. Smith!'

❋

Our first visitors, Colonel L. R. Moore and his wife, slept in the hotel on 1st March, 1910. Until very recently they were regular guests from Devon and very proud of their connection with the Goring Hotel. They do not visit us any more, for I believe Colonel Moore is bedridden. However, they sent us a long letter on the occasion of our golden jubilee.

❋

One night in 1916 I looked out of my bedroom window and saw an enormous burning 'cigar' in the sky. It was the raiding Zeppelin which crashed at Potters Bar, some fifteen miles away.

❋

Situated within 100 yards of Buckingham Palace, the Goring

Hotel has been called 'the little annexe to Buckingham Palace'. Such a description is surely a very honourable distinction.

It is a fact that during any special function at Buckingham Palace the Goring Hotel, over these last thirty years, has been asked to co-operate in the question of supplying accommodation. Thus for the last three Coronations suites of rooms—in fact, almost whole floors—have been set aside for visiting Royalty and their entourage from Europe, and all accounts are rendered to the Lord Chamberlain.

During the Coronation of King George VI we had the then Crown Prince of Denmark with his Consort as our guests. As usual on these occasions, the hotel had a private telephone wire connected to Buckingham Palace. Footmen in Royal scarlet were supplied by the Master of the King's Household and stationed at the entries to the suites occupied by royal guests. The road from the hotel to the Palace was closed and patrolled by police at certain times of the day. These footmen were mostly old Palace retainers brought in from retirement for these occasions of extraordinary duties. One day the Crown Prince, with several important guests, had a private luncheon party. The butler, in scarlet, in attendance with my regular staff, presented the menu to the Crown Prince with a stub end of a very dirty and bitten pencil, with the remark 'Ere you are. Mark it orf.' Thank goodness I was in the room at the time and able to make amends. The incident raised a hearty laugh from the Crown Prince, however.

Similarly, every state visit, be it from Denmark, France, Italy, Germany, Holland, or any other country, brings requests for accommodation for the various important officials not actually housed in Buckingham Palace. Our Coronation Panel, situated in the front hall, is reproduced opposite page 128.

Likewise, our Visitors' Book, which is only brought out on special occasions, is a memento of those many world personalities who have actually stayed at the Goring.

The signatures, covering many pages, include that of Sir Winston Churchill, K.G., O.M., M.P. who lived at the Goring Hotel with his family for several months in 1937.

Sir Austen Chamberlain, K.G., our great senior statesman of the period between the wars, lived for two years at the Goring. During the period of sanctions against Italy in 1935, Anthony

Eden (now Sir) often called to see him in those days of anxiety during the Italo-Abyssinian War.

Great generals, famous admirals, politicians, ambassadors, and innumerable titled people have made the Goring Hotel their headquarters from time to time.

My list of the many English titled people who stayed at the hotel between the wars totals over 400.

Trygve Lye, the first Secretary-General of U.N.O., was a very regular guest. In fact, he received his appointment while staying at the Goring. A very considerate man, he always brought me presents of choice cheese, caviar, *foie gras*, or some such tasty fancy on his many trips to London, when we were still suffering from rationing after the war.

*

I am proud to recognize the high standard of comfort and refinement the Goring Hotel has achieved. So highly are our services esteemed that a certain British Ambassador to Moscow entrusted us with the purchase of foodstuffs to fill a large deep-freeze he had had constructed at the British Embassy there. We sent a consignment by charter plane, including sirloins of Scotch beef, lamb, mutton, hams, potted shrimps, shellfish, cream, special cheeses, and other items to vary the monotony, and to show the Soviet rulers the type of food we were used to over here. I feel sure that Anglo-Soviet relations were improved by this tactful way of changing the menu on important diplomatic occasions.

*

In 1927 the first wireless transmission to America came into operation from a station at Rugby. The experimental work took place at the Goring Hotel. One day a large double bedroom was booked by two Americans, who proceeded to install a frightening amount of wireless equipment. These two gentlemen were top-line engineers from the Edison Bell Co. of America, and a day or two before their departure the Rugby Relay Station was inaugurated.

*

A noble peer, a visitor of very many years, standing (known to us as a collector of international personalities), had a special luncheon party during the war. His guests were Noel Baker, Pierre Cot, and King Haille Selassie of Abyssinia.

I told Chef what sort of menu I wanted. Chef replied: 'For Pierre Cot . . . for that *sale bête* . . . I do nothing. *J'aimerais mieux lui tuer.*' However, the lunch was a great success.

Months later, Pierre Cot came again, with a party. I told Chef, 'Now here's your chance to poison Pierre Cot—your *bête noire*, Chef replied: 'Perhaps it is better not. I might get deported.'

*

Sir Reginald Wingate, Sirdar (ruler) of Egypt from 1899 to 1916, and High Commissioner in Egypt from 1917 to 1919, was not only a visitor of long standing at the Goring Hotel, but actually lived with us during the War of 1939-45. Naturally, we became very friendly, and many a chat we had about Egypt at the time that Wingate and Kitchener subdued the Mahdi uprising and took Khartoum.

One day in 1941 Sir Reginald Wingate told me that during his term of office early in the century he had travelled by camel from Cairo to Tobruk, and he knew the area of the Eighth Army operations very well indeed. He explained at length and with emphasis that at the end of the nineteenth century a young naval lieutenant had reported to him the obvious advantage of Tobruk as a port to be acquired 'for future use' by H.M. (Queen Victoria) as a first-class naval base in the Mediterranean, equal to Malta.

Wingate even went to look at this natural (but uninhabited) port and was so impressed that he obtained a personal interview with Queen Victoria, stressing the advisability of taking over the harbour 'in the name of the British Government'.

Queen Victoria would have appeared to reply: 'I am sorry. The coastline of North Africa comes under the jurisdiction of our friends the Turks, and we would be ill advised to start a controversy with one of our allies.'

Had Wingate had his way on that occasion, the Eighth Army battles might never have been fought, for in the 1914-18 War Turkey was our enemy and in the 1939-45 War Turkey was neutral. If we had held Tobruk from 1895 onwards the desert campaign of 1940-3 might have been avoided.

During his term as Sirdar of Egypt at the end of the last century, Sir Reginald Wingate went to Abyssinia (now Ethiopia) on a goodwill mission. Very friendly relations existed at that time between Queen Victoria and the Emperor of Abyssinia. So much so that the Empress of Abyssinia showed the famous necklace of the Queen of Sheba—that fabulous necklace—to Sir Reginald. The Empress asked if H.M. Queen Victoria would like a copy of it. Sir Reginald, naturally, said, 'Yes, please.'

So precious is the Queen of Sheba's necklace that nobody is allowed even to touch it. A strict ritual of Coronation ceremonies, Royal weddings, etc., is tied up with the use of this world-famous, fabulous necklace, which actually exists, although it is kept well away from public gaze.

The talented silversmith who copied the necklace was not allowed by Royal protocol to handle it, and the Empress had to hold it the whole time whilst the silversmith took his dimensions and drawings. Sir Reginald is one of the very few white people who have been privileged to see this priceless necklace.

When it was completed Sir Reginald obtained leave of absence from the Near East and took the copy necklace personally to H.M. Queen Victoria at Balmoral, where he enjoyed the Queen's hospitality for some days. In fact, on many occasions he was a guest and adviser to Her Majesty on matters concerning Egypt and the Sudan, then under British rule.

Having lived at the Goring Hotel during the war period, Sir Reginald retired to his estate in Scotland, and, as Lady Wingate had died about that time, he was looked after by his niece.

'Looked after' is possibly a wrong expression, for in 1947 he came to visit us at our country estate at Wrotham. At that time I was Chairman of the local Boy Scouts Group in our part of Kent and, as all good Scouters know, we have a March Past on the Sunday following St. George's Day. Sir Reginald Wingate honoured us by taking the Scouts' March Past on this occasion, attending the special Scouts' Church Service and addressing the combined troops of Scouts afterwards. Our West Malling Scout Group (Kent) has a Wingate Trophy in memory of the occasion.

The old gentleman was in about his eightieth year at the time of his visit to our home. My sons (twins) were then about twelve years old. They were naturally thrilled at having such an important guest staying in our house, and Sir Reginald played his part very nobly indeed. For the Scouts' March Past the old gentleman had brought his dress uniform and all his medals—about three rows of them—and proceeded to explain to my boys the meaning of each medal in turn.

Then, to their great delight, he proceeded to play cat's-cradle with string for their entertainment. Not the ordinary line of cat's-cradle, but manipulations with string which were very much more complicated, a real conjurer's repertoire.

What a marvellous character that man had—from the very highest heights as Governor of Egypt to playing cat's-cradle at the age of eighty plus.

A really great but simple man—a friend and contemporary of Baden Powell, Kitchener, Buller, Queen Victoria, King Edward VII and King George V. How proud I am to be able to call him a friend!

*

Orde Wingate, the famous Chindit leader in the fight against the Japanese in South-East Asia, is said to have come home to England to meet H.M. King George VI to make a report on conditions in that territory at the time. He is said to have flown from India in his short—somewhat dirty—jungle kit. Some people believed this to be 'newspaper talk'. It is actually true. Orde Wingate arrived in London at 11.30 one morning in dirty kit (unworthy of an officer), had lunch at the Goring Hotel with his uncle, Sir Reginald Wingate, and went straight from the hotel to Buckingham Palace. We all realize that he was a very fine—if eccentric—soldier, and his appearance at the Goring Hotel certainly caused comment at the time. What the King thought of his appearance at Buckingham Palace is not my concern. He was unfortunately killed in a plane crash shortly afterwards.

Admiral Fountaine was a very regular visitor to the Goring Hotel during the period between the wars. He owned a house in Norfolk with over 100 rooms and he was proud of the fact that a spring of water actually flowed from under his dining-room to form the main waters of the largest river in Norfolk.

*

Visitors

Between the wars we had a very regular visitor who came to lunch every day and had his offices exactly opposite the hotel in Grosvenor Gardens.

He was the Chairman of Quasi-Arc, and his firm experimented with welded ships. Up to this time all ships had their sides-plates riveted. This gentleman, however, built a ship with its hull plates welded one to another, in the present-day fashion. He met a lot of opposition from the Clyde and Tyne, on the assumption that welded ships were too rigid and would not 'give' in the stress of a storm. To prove his beliefs, he had to build a ship and put it to sea for twenty years before Lloyd's would pass it as A1 for insurance. During the First World War his firm was employed in building 'bulges' on battleships to counteract the effect of torpedoes. His offices in Grosvenor Gardens became so over-burdened with Government papers and documents that the two top floors showed signs of giving way under the weight. Apart from correspondence with the Admiralty, every conversation with a naval official had to be recorded.

His ship, of course, passed its A1 risk test at Lloyd's after twenty years at sea, and his process of shipbuilding is common practice today.

His advanced ideas received no recognition from any Government department. Worse still was the fate of his son. In the basement of their office block in Grosvenor Gardens was a very powerful X-ray plant which was used to test steel for flaws and defects. Kenneth was in charge of this plant, which, because of its powerful reactions, was contained in a strong-room lined with leaded walls. Familiarity breeds contempt, however, and Kenneth did not always take the precautions for his safety that he should have done. Thus he got an X-ray complaint akin to polio. I saw him about two years ago at a Guild dinner in the city—in an invalid chair—having lost the use of his legs. Here again his services to the nation went unseen and unrewarded.

*

The great wartime theatre distraction, *Me and My Girl*, was played at the Victoria Palace for many years during the war. As we all remember, the Lambeth Walk, with Lupino Lane, took the world (even Russia) by storm. Incidentally, the play was *nearly* taken off, after only two weeks, before the war broke out. It was considered 'just not good enough'. Lupino Lane and his manager, Mr. Rose, got the main theme songs put over the wireless and the play was made. This was one of the first wireless broadcasts straight from the stage, and was frowned upon by both the

B.B.C. and the stage people as likely to interfere with each other's interests. I happened to listen to this short B.B.C. programme and at once went to buy some tickets. I never laughed so much in my life, and I gave the show a five-year run. I was right!

During the war years, Lupino Lane often stayed with his wife (his leading lady) at the Goring, for he had difficulty in getting back home to the suburbs in the black-out. Towards the end of the war he used to come staggering home from the Victoria Palace, 300 yards away, through Victoria Square, and we usually had a final drink together. One night I said, 'No; not tonight, Lupino. It's bed for you.' His wife was with him that night and at once jumped to his defence. 'It's not that, Mr. Goring,' she said. 'Have you seen his legs?' She proceeded to pull up his trousers to knee height and displayed his legs, burnt and bandaged to above the knee. He must have suffered agonies on the stage for several months.

Incidentally, Lupino Lane was very shy when off-stage. On one occasion the Westminster Rotary Club arranged a competition, and he came to give away the prize, which concerned his own activities at the Victoria Palace. His nervousness and stuttering were extremely noticeable when presenting the prize, which was a blue fox stole.

Lupino Lane, during the course of his activities each evening on the stage in *Me and My Girl*, appeared to cover several miles during each act. The competition was to assess exactly what distance he did actually walk (apart from walking backwards and turning somersaults). For this test he very sportingly consented to wearing a pedometer to calculate the distance covered. He was impressed himself at the true mileage involved.

*

At that time, travel each day to our small country house being difficult—for we were four miles from a railway station and petrol was rationed—we kept our very sophisticated Siamese cat (against all house rules) in our flat in the hotel. This was the flat that Lupino Lane used to visit.

Our Siamese cat—named Sheba—just could not stand the presence of Mrs. Lupino Lane, who herself was allergic to cats. Sheba was always docile and very well-behaved, and never left our flat except to go out of the window into the garden. Twice, however, when Mrs. Lupino Lane was present, she dashed upstairs growling, and was very difficult to retrieve until the said lady had gone upstairs to bed. Once we caught her on the second floor and once on the fourth floor, and each time we brought her back she immediately tried to escape again.

I know cats are allergic to those who do not like them, but this display was surely more marked than in most cases.

There are two ways of bringing up cats. One is to play with them roughly, to which a cat will respond roughly. The proper way, of course, is to play with a cat gently—that is to say, do not tease it too much and do not pull your hand away sharply when playing. To pull your hand away sharply makes a cat 'snatch' at your hand with claws open, as if instinctively trying to catch a mouse. It is a cat's nature. So, if one never 'snatches' away from a cat, that cat will always be gentle.

I remember one evening a very important gentleman came into our flat and started to play rough with our Sheba. We warned him not to 'snatch' her, but he insisted on doing so. Sheba thought: 'Well, if you want to play rough, I don't mind. I can play rough also!' After a few minutes Sheba got the idea—and pulled a beautiful full-claw scratch right down his nose—five lovely lines of blood. The gentleman in question—Chairman of an important institute—had to make a speech that evening. We have often ragged him about it since!

*

Just after the war was over we entertained a Dr. Citrine, son of the well-known Labour politician. He had been with a party of four other young medicos to Belsen, and had seen all the horrors of that appalling camp. He just 'opened out', and my wife and I feel sure that to this day he remembers his outburst and his vivid description of the terrible things he saw there, for it relieved his nerves and obviously acted as an escape from his experiences.

*

It is a well-known fact that those unfortunate men who had been interned in P.O.W. camps took a long time to overcome the thoughts of their experiences and rehabilitate themselves. One such young man, a South African and the son of a very well-known and rich family, came to stay at the Goring Hotel

E

soon after his release. He had been in London for three weeks
ostensibly working as British representative for his father's firm
in South Africa. He had no interest in life, no thoughts, no
conversation. He was entirely uprooted—as indeed were so many
who endured long periods in those terrible camps.

My wife and I 'got him talking' one night after a couple of
strong drinks. He talked and cried for about two hours, but it
cured him. This experience was common to very many ex-
P.O.Ws. Once one could 'break them down' and get them to
talk, the major part of their trouble was over, and they returned
to a normal mental outlook on 'civvy street' prospects.

*

Muffins once caused me a little trouble. Muffins and crumpets
are available in the southern counties of England only between
the months of September and April. Outside that period they
are 'out of season'.

An American visitor once came to the hotel in July, and he
insisted on muffins for breakfast. I telephoned a number of
bakers, only to receive the reply I expected—'Sorry. Out of
season.'

My wife, a Yorkshire woman, reminded me that muffin shops
keep open the year round in Yorkshire: they have to sell something or shut down, as they are specialists. So I sent to a firm
in Sheffield and obtained muffins by return. My visitor never
knew that he had transgressed the 'muffin season', and that his
muffins had been acquired 170 miles away.

*

Between the wars Admiral Sir Arthur Gough-Calthorpe was
a very regular visitor to the Goring Hotel. One day, shortly
before his retirement, he asked me up to his sitting-room to
witness his signature to a very important and legal-looking
document, which, naturally, I was pleased to do. Having signed,
he proceeded to show me the document, which was nothing
more or less than the reassignment of the whole of Portsmouth
Dockyard to his successor. I did not know—and I suspect that
very many of my readers do not realize—that an Admiral-in-
Charge, Home Command, is assigned the deeds of such a
valuable piece of Government property, worth millions of

pounds, during the period of his command. The responsibility must be very great.

*

Talking of admirals, the son of a famous titled Admiral of First World War fame was also a constant visitor to the Goring. Lord and Lady Fisher and their (then) young family were friendly people and I often had long conversations with them. His Lordship, who was a farmer on a very large and successful scale, lived at Thetford in Norfolk. He complained bitterly to me one evening about the noisy lorries passing his house at 2 a.m. each day, taking agricultural produce to Covent Garden Market in London. They kept him awake. Actually, he was one of the accepted best producers of blackcurrants in Great Britain. I asked him how he marketed his fruit in view of the price fluctuations in the different parts of England. He replied, 'Oh, I phone up the various market centres in the afternoon to ascertain the best prices. Sometimes I switch from Covent Garden to Cardiff overnight. Of course, I get a lorry out at about midnight to make the market in time for the next morning!'

Incidentally, the asparagus grown on his estates was about the best in England. He marketed it in Covent Garden under his own name, and his bundles always got the top prices for specially graded produce.

In 1914 he 'put down' a Stilton cheese to be kept until the peace celebrations. In 1918, at Christmas, the Mayor and local celebrities were called together at a thanksgiving celebration to 'cut the cheese'. I believe this event is still remembered by the old inhabitants of Thetford! Anyhow, some of them enjoyed the cheese.

One day I was talking to this same noble Lord, who was having luncheon with his family. He was eating cheese, and called me over to his table. 'Which of these cheeses is the best, Mr. Goring?' he asked. At once his (now married) daughter, then about fourteen years old, chipped in before anyone else could think: 'The answer is *Stilton*, Mr. Goring.'

Towards the end of the Coronation ceremony of King George VI rain fell heavily in London. Lord and Lady Fisher were, naturally, seated in Westminster Abbey. Their family, however, were not so fortunate and they came back to the hotel very wet indeed, having walked home.

Their elder son, then about sixteen years of age, had extremely wet feet. His father noticed this, and the boy said, 'I'm just going up to my bedroom to take my shoes off and give them to the hotel valet to have dried for me.'

'You are doing nothing of the sort, my boy', replied Father. 'You are taking them off here in the front hall, and are taking them down yourself to the boiler-house—wherever that might be—just as you've been taught to do at home.'

*

Two or three days before that Coronation, I received a request from two well-known gentlemen to prepare them a packed lunch to take to Westminster Abbey. I suggested the usual wrapped sandwiches, champagne, or whisky and soda, etc.

I was told that the sandwiches must be wrapped in a napkin, with no paper around them. Champagne was out of the question, as the cork might pop off. Soda was impossible, as it would fizz. Glasses could not be used, as one could hear liquid being poured into them. We settled on very soft sandwiches and special containers of sweetened tea. I was thanked for the trouble I had taken over this unusual request. The two gentlemen concerned were the B.B.C. commentators responsible for the world broadcast over the wireless. They had a special 'box' in the roof of Westminster Abbey, and any noise of champagne corks or whisky and soda might be heard all over the world!

*

Up to a few years ago the use of a crest or armorial bearings was taxed by the Government. During the First World War, when the hotel was commandeered, our hotel crest was not used. After about three years of non-use, my father suddenly realized that he had been paying tax on armorial bearings although the hotel was closed. He wrote, on hotel notepaper, to the appropriate authority, requesting a refund, only to receive a reply to the effect that as the notepaper on which he had written bore the said crest, it could not be an absolute fact that the said armorial bearings had not been in use.

*

The Rev. Brian Hession was another interesting character whom my wife and I got to know well just before the war.

In those days 'talkies' were just being shown at the cinemas, which had late houses up to about midnight—in fact, it was at this period that the cinema craze reached its height.

We used to go to the Metropole Cinema, Victoria, each week, and soon became acquainted with Brian Hession, who was then absorbed in a cinema version of *The Life of Christ*. This was shown in sections after midnight, with an audience of the author, my wife, the cinema Manager, Mr. Sowden, and myself. The theme was too ambitious and came to nothing, the main stumbling-block being the attitude of the Church towards the portrayal of Christ Himself as an individual. However, the evenings were most instructive in this vast cinema hall built to hold 2,000 people with just the four of us present.

Brian, unfortunately, became smitten with cancer shortly afterwards, and had to give up work for some time.

When I next saw him, after the war, he was enthusiastic on 'still' slides used for educational lectures.

He then bought an hotel near Bournemouth, which he still operates, and despite his extremely bad health he is able to ski in Switzerland, continue his interest in film work, and also run his country-house hotel. As happens so often in these cases, he is extremely active and looks at least ten years younger than his real age.

*

Arthur Mee, that household name in all families with children, lived at the Goring Hotel from 1920 until shortly before his illness, and death, around 1938. When I say 'lived', I should have said 'had a room'. He spent five days a week with us and went down to his charming house at Eynesford, Kent, every week-end to be with his family.

He, naturally, had an inquisitive mind and was interested in anything new, as was to be expected from a man with such a wonderful gift for telling the thousands of facts about the world to children of under prep.-school age. His gift in this direction was remarkable.

After the Boer War he edited a large monthly periodical entitled *The Children's Encyclopaedia*, subscribed to by tens of thousands of parents and read by hundreds of thousands of children. In those days the parents were proud to be able to answer the many inquisitive questions which children asked, and they obtained their information largely through Arthur Mee. Today, with the progress of education, they are, by and large, not so interested.

Every spring the copies issued during the previous year were bound into a volume, which graced the bookshelves of all and sundry. This monumental work appeared year after year, and really was a résumé of the world's activities in every sphere of life, covering the last 4,000 years.

Later, before the First World War, the title was changed. I still have several volumes of this newer work, dated 1911-14, entitled *The Children's Magazine*—being a continuation of *The Children's Encyclopaedia*. Edited by Arthur Mee, and published by the Amalgamated Press, London, each bound volume—of about 700 pages—gave facts of the world, arranged monthly, to cover every known subject. For instance, general knowledge (over 300), with articles on Jack's House (6), literature (26), music (6), nature calendar (15), picture galleries (47), photographs (16), poetry (75), stories, chiefly with simple educational bias (220), why things are done (40), and so on. These figures are taken roughly from Volume 6 of *The Children's Magazine*—issued over a period of about six months—and they show what a terrific scope and diversity of knowledge was let loose on the young people through Arthur Mee.

I asked Arthur Mee one day how on earth all this knowledge was obtainable by one man. He replied, 'I have no knowledge, but I know how to find it.' Of course, he had many paid people who supplied his résumé of this world's work.

So far as I am aware, Arthur Mee only had one daughter, whom I met on many occasions. He should have had a family of at least ten, judging by his love of children, shown through his writings.

He did everything with the child mentally in front of him. His *A Thousand Beautiful Things* and his *Children's Bible* come to mind as to his real love of children.

When I married, and my family came into being, he said to me one day: 'You see, Goring, I now have three more prospective customers for my books!' I replied: 'No, Arthur, you are wrong, for I still have your *Children's Magazine* from 1911-14, which I can hand down to the family in due course and thus save my subscription.' He did not like this approach of mine, for I had understood for many years that the *Magazine* was a rehash of *The Children's Encyclopaedia*, and that the series running in the 1930s was again a rehash of *The Children's Magazine*. He had the good grace to admit that I was 'about right'.

I have mentioned above that Arthur Mee was inquisitive by instinct. To prove this I can state that in 1922 he already had a wireless (crystal set) installed in his room, No. 38, at the Goring Hotel. Such a marvellous invention, bringing voices and music 'out of the air', was little known to the general public at that time. His set was primitive, but it worked, and many a time, as a young man, I went up to room No. 38 to listen in with head-phones.

It was thus that I learned that the midnight chimes of Big Ben come across the wireless (even a crystal set) faster than the actual chimes reach us at the Goring Hotel.

We are just under one mile away, in a direct line, from Big Ben. Room No. 38 faces towards the south-east in the direction of Big Ben. On the 'Close-down' or 'Midnight chime', we definitely got the wireless relay of Big Ben one stroke early. In other words, after the wireless had relayed twelve strokes from Big Ben at midnight, the actual twelfth stroke came to us across the atmosphere one beat late. With modern wireless, B.B.C., T.V., I.T.V., A.T.V., etc., this is still a fact, and I claim we are the only hotel in the world where such a phenomenon takes place every night of the year. At midday the normal traffic of London does not allow the sound of Big Ben to penetrate to the Goring Hotel, but the same effect is present if traffic noise is stopped.

The speed of sound is such that the hours of ten or eleven do not have this effect of an 'echo in reverse'. Other private houses at our exact distance radius from Big Ben probably could get the same effect, but I doubt if any of them realize it.

I visited Arthur Mee's house at Eynesford on more than one occasion. His house was surrounded by a large estate, sloping uphill. At the top of the hill he had excavated the remains of a real Roman villa, mosaic floors and all—which was typical of the man.

He had, also, in his study a window niche, fitted with a window-seat. Under this seat was a small white cupboard, and inside this cupboard was a crystal wireless receiving set, which was capable of picking up Morse signals in the English Channel

long before the First World War. I believe that he got into
trouble for using this receiving set during that war, for being in
communication with war-time shipping. This particular set was
still working as late as 1932.

Later, just before he gave up active life, he edited a series of
county histories, on which the handsome sum of £29,000 was
being spent. He finished London, Derbyshire, and Lincoln,
but ill-health made him give up this ambitious series. I formed
the opinion at the time that this particular series was virtually a
rehash of *Kelly's County Directories*, with the names and history
of the various village churches in each county.

*

Convocations of Lambeth hold a particular interest for the
Goring Hotel. In 1948 we were honoured by the visit of eleven
American bishops, accompanied by their wives and/or families,
as the case was.

This Convocation, taking place during the summer months
and lasting about six weeks, gave me an excellent opportunity
to ask these guests down to my country estate—which, incidentally, covers many acres and provides all the flowers and a lot
of the vegetables used at the Goring Hotel. The house itself is
early Georgian and is a perfect specimen of the 1750 period, with
a bow façade facing south and a rounded dome which obviously
contained a telescope in days gone by, when 'star-gazing' was a
fashionable and useful accomplishment. Another interesting
fact is that Jane Austen wrote *Pride and Prejudice* in what is now
our morning-room.

It is astonishing that these bishops staying at the Goring
Hotel, as well as very very many others from different parts of
the globe, had not previously been asked to a private house
party. They had all been invited to endless official luncheons,
teas, dinners, receptions, etc., but not to a private house in the
country where they could meet the average better-class and
'county' families—which really make up the backbone of our
country.

The names and titles of these bishops are inscribed in our
Visitors' Book, and I know they enjoyed the afternoon and
evening with us.

In fact, so successful was our effort in 1948 that we decided to make the same gesture during the Convocation of Lambeth in 1958. Our 1948 effort had 'snowballed' to such advantage that in 1958 we had twenty-three American bishops and their wives staying at the Goring Hotel.

Here again I noted that very few of them had been asked to a real English country house to meet our local and county people. They had obviously been through the gambit of 'functions' of the official type. In 1958, therefore, we entertained twenty-three American and Canadian bishops at my country home at Court Lodge, Wrotham, Kent. About 100 'locals' were invited to meet them.

An American bishop is a little different from an English bishop, although they may belong to the same Church. Your American bishop is very much the business-man, and seems to understand the requirements of his diocese to a marked degree. American bishops also speak English. By this I mean that of the twenty-three bishops who were our guests, there was not one who spoke with an American or any other sort of accent. Frankly, this surprised—and very much pleased—me.

Their sense of humour—always useful—was remarkable. I hired ten private cars from London to convey my guests to Wrotham. One bishop said to me, 'I did not know—with this long procession of cars—whether you were really going to entertain us at your private house or if I was going to my own funeral.'

Another American Bishop said that one of his parishioners 'way back home' had asked him how he prepared holy water. He had a snappy reply. He said, 'Oh! Just boil the Hell out of it.'

CHAPTER SIX

Menu and Kitchen Trends

SINCE the Goring Hotel opened in 1910 the feeding habits of the upper class people have altered very considerably. During the reign of Edward VII, six-course luncheons and seven-course dinners were the order of the day. At that time too, the garnishing and presentation of dishes was at its highest level. Dishes of meat or fish would be presented at the table as veritable works of art, and a great deal of time was spent in every hotel kitchen in the actual work of making a dish look pretty and well-garnished—an art which has unfortunately died out today with the enormous increase in kitchen wages, the indifference of the public, and the speed at which meals must be served in this mid-twentieth century. In those days the enjoyment of a meal was for the eye as well as the palate. Speed of service was not encouraged, while the presentation of the various artistically presented dishes was very much appreciated.

The job of a chef (or a brigade of cooks in an hotel) was, therefore, more leisurely, but at the same time more exacting.

The Edwardian era was also the champagne era. King Edward VII liked champagne, and champagne only, during the course of his meal; so the upper classes took to drinking it. He was right, in my opinion, for too many mixtures of various wines at a meal leaves one with a bad palate, not only at the time but the next morning also. Champagne drunk right through a meal leaves a clean taste in the mouth and does not associate itself with a 'hangover'. Let it be said that champagne cost only about £1 bottle. At official club or association functions the seven-course meal was interspersed with considerable vocal entertainment from raconteurs, singers (both sexes), pianists, and others. In those days of slower service, before hotel kitchens became so highly equipped, the object was to mask the time-lag between the courses by a short turn.

Menus were printed on very small cards and in such small print as to be almost unreadable. The outside of the menu card would have the name of the society or club. Inside on the left would be a long list of the dishes to be served, divided by a line showing the very considerable choice of wines to be imbibed. Inside on the right would be the equally long list of speakers to propose and respond to each toast, followed by a list of entertainers.

During the First World War these long menus were very much curtailed. In the first place we had rationing, which, obviously, altered our habits of eating and drinking. Menus became more simple and rationing coupons had to be collected for each item served. I still have some rationing books referring to the 1914-18 War, and I have also the Rationing Returns Books for the Goring Hotel, which contained the allowed quantities of food (meat, fat, milk, butter, etc.) which were allowed to our establishment each week. In that war coupons had to be clipped off by the waiter serving the meal in a restaurant, and a very awkward and unsatisfactory system it was.

Having had the experience of war, we found that by 1922 the food situation had become normal. So back we went to a five-course luncheon and a seven-course dinner.

Champagne as a sole accompaniment went out of fashion, for taxes put champagne at a very much higher level, allowing red and white wines from France and Germany to take its place, with champagne served only towards the end of a meal.

Please do not believe that ordinary red and white table wines went completely out of the picture. They did not, but champagne had its heyday during the reign of King Edward VII.

Entertaining during the course of a meal became less prevalent and consisted of only one raconteur or singer, instead of the veritable music-hall show at the turn of the century.

Thus things continued until 1939 and the outbreak of the last war. Again food rationing came into force, but a food rationing based on common sense. Each establishment was allowed an assessed quantity of eggs, meat, sugar, tea, butter, fats, cheese, etc., based on the number of meals served. Fortunately, fish was uncontrolled. The allocation for each establishment was checked against the number of meals served, and the allocation could go up or down, according to business demands.

The question of main meals as against subsidiary meals was also controlled. A main meal, generally speaking, was luncheon or dinner, at which meat would be normally served. A subsidiary meal consisted of afternoon tea, sandwiches, etc., while breakfasts were controlled on a separate form. Our allocation of eggs, for example, was sixty-five per week at one period. Eggs and bacon were, therefore, quite impossible at breakfast (bacon, 14 lb. per week, including gammon), and many substitutes were 'invented'. Our normal purchase of eggs before the war was 1,000 eggs a week, and now after controls were released it is at least 2,000 eggs per week.

So fish, fish-cakes, fried potato-cakes, muffins, etc., all took the place of eggs and bacon. This continued until long after the war.

During all this period a meal was confined to three courses: one first course (*hors d'œuvre*, soup, or farinaceous dishes), a main course of meat or poultry, followed by a course of pudding or cheese. As cheese was rationed, there was not very much of it available. A maximum price of 5s. per person was imposed. Certain first-class London establishments, however, were allowed a supplementary price according to pre-war cooking standards and overheads. The Goring Hotel was fortunately among them.

The ingenuity of some of the big food-manufacturing firms became a feature of those days, and caterers still thank these firms for their efforts. Powdered egg, powdered milk, powdered potatoes, cake-mixes, etc., all hardly known to us before the war, were stepped up in production. In fact, war conditions stimulated the vast increase in processed foods as we understand them today.

A fillet of veal fried in breadcrumbs is a delightful dish, as we all know. But veal was absolutely unobtainable during the war. We soon found out that rabbit legs, boned and breadcrumbed, formed an excellent substitute, equally as wholesome. Unfortunately one gets two portions per rabbit. This became a little expensive, as the rest of the animal had to be used in pies or for stews. I nearly got into trouble at one time, for I was reported to the food authorities for serving veal—apparently obtained from an unknown blackmarket—and had to explain my rabbit (uncontrolled) activities to the Food Control Authorities who, being without culinary knowledge, were inclined to query my explanation. Edible horse-meat and whale-meat helped to relieve the monotony in some establishments.

Now that the war is well in the background these things are nearly forgotten, but they certainly caused us headaches at the time. All this leads up to the fact that the British public takes meals of fewer courses today, which may be healthier for them: luncheon, three courses; dinner, four to five courses.

Looking back on fifty years of service, one is surprised at the improvement in catering conditions. Up to 1926 the Goring was equipped with only one large ice-box in which to keep meat, fish, milk, etc., in good condition. It inevitably resulted in the fact that a great quantity of raw foodstuff went 'off' during the hot weather. Fish used to be kept actually 'on the ice' in order to retain its freshness and moisture. Large joints of meat used to be kept 'as near as possible' in the 'ice-safe', as it was called. Of course, milk and butter, two of the most delicate foodstuffs we handle, were very tricky and caused endless trouble. Sour milk and rancid butter were a constant source of anxiety. Occasions arose when some clot of a waiter took ice, on which fish had been resting; probably too lazy to wash it, he proceeded to put the fishy ice into a cocktail-shaker!

This is just one example of the many mistakes which could be made, and for which the management was responsible.

Gas and electricity largely control our kitchens of today, and a lot of hard labour and dirt has thus been eliminated.

With the advent of infra-red electric grills, the service has also been speeded up. Instead of ordering your chop or steak twenty minutes ahead, it can now be ordered at the table and served within five minutes in perfect condition as 'rare', 'medium', or 'well-cooked'.

The service of wines and spirits has also improved by refrigeration. White wines in particular should be kept at an even, cool temperature all the year round, or the wine will suffer. The central, or main, cellar is normally in the basement in a cool spot, so that it is not affected. It is at the dispense, a small issue room used as a shop for the wine service staff, near the pantry or service room and near the kitchen heat, that the trouble starts.

For many years the Goring had a big ice cupboard, properly racked and binned, for the storage of white wines and mineral waters at the proper cool temperatures. In fact, there were not many establishments in Great Britain which could boast of such a convenience at that time. At the top—6 feet up—was a large metal-lined ice-box, complete with wooden slats, draining pipes, trays, and other gadgets to carry away the melted ice into a nearby sink. For the information of the reader it should be stated that melted ice does not return to pure water—it produces a jelly-like substance which blocks the water-release pipes. To overcome this we had a rubber blow-pipe fitted, to clear the discharge water as and when required. And do not forget that this large wine-cooling device had to be filled with 5 cwt. of block ice each day, brought by hand from the basement and lifted 6 feet into position. This wine-cooling cabinet still exists— but the old ice-box now contains an up-to-date freezing unit, which is so much more efficient in all respects.

*

I have often been asked how we in the hotel industry can calculate ahead the number of meals and the type of food that we shall be expected to serve at any one time.

To my mind, brought up in the business, this is a simple question. It is in fact so simple that I cannot answer it!

Of course, one knows in advance of any special functions that are booked, the number of people expected for these functions, and the menu desired. Apart from this, the day-to-day business is largely ruled by the law of averages. Say we expect an average 100 people in the restaurant for luncheon from Monday to Friday: we know that that number will fall to about sixty at the week-end. Say that there is a choice of six dishes on the 'main course' menu: we know that of the average 100 lunches served, our guests will choose 30 per cent. a 'cut off the joint', 15 per cent. fish, 20 per cent. a good made-up dish, 10 per cent. an omelette or eggs, 10 per cent. cold meats, and 15 per cent. a personal à la carte choice.

We also know that certain dishes are more popular than others. For instance, joints and grills apart, we know that steak and kidney pudding (or pie), chicken pie, chicken curry, boiled salt silverside, boiled fresh beef, oxtail garnished, and liver and bacon are all popular dishes, and we make allowances accordingly. We are, of course, helped by the fact that modern refrigeration does away with the necessity to 'pre-cook' food, which might otherwise be wasted.

The general public seems to have a rooted objection to made-up dishes. Take a Hamburg steak (minced beef) as an example. So often have I heard from friends (not at the Goring Hotel), 'Oh, that's a made-up dish—all the old left-overs!' This is a complete fallacy, for a good Hamburg steak must be made from freshly minced beef or it will not hold together properly and be palatable.

I quote only the one example.

My chef, who has been with me for upwards of twenty years now, and I are always having talks on this subject of made-up dishes. They are often very much better than a straight cut off a joint or a mutton chop, for they show the art of the cook, and so often take a much longer time to prepare.

I am always saying, 'Change these —— menus. Always the same monotony of dishes.'

Chef has given way to me on many occasions in this matter and has made some really first-class luncheon dishes just a little out of the ordinary. He has spent time and imagination on these dishes, and my head waiter has tried to support him by recommending these dishes to our guests. I know they have been good, yet the total number taken by our guests is generally only about 6-10 per cent. I mention this because some people say that British cooking is 'all the same—no imagination'. It is not the cooks, it is the general public that has no imagination.

*

There is a lot in the creating of a new dish, and the variety of dishes is so great today that it is difficult to find something outstandingly new.

Escoffier in England, of course, was the first great master chef of this century to write an encyclopaedia on recipes, and he has been followed by others.

A few years ago, for a £5 bet, I issued a challenge to anyone who could tell me the recipe for *poulet à la King*. I got no replies, and my £5 is still in my pocket.

Poulet à la King is a supreme *de poulet sous cloche*, covered with a white supreme sauce flavoured with whisky, and garnished with pimentos cut in strips. It has nothing to do with royalty, and was a recipe prepared at the old Carlton Hotel in London by Escoffier, who was *Maître Chef* there at that time. The recipe was sent down to Escoffier by an American guest in the restaurant (about 1910). At first Escoffier demurred at being taught his own business by a 'mere' restaurant customer. He pleased his customer, however, whose name was 'Mr. King'. Hence *poulet à la King*.

There are only three people active today who remember the incident, one of whom is my own chef, Mr. Gasc, who was working at the Carlton Hotel in a very junior position in the kitchens at the time. I have had many versions of *poulet à la King* served to me from time to time, in many different countries, but never the right one.

Unlike the *Pharmaceutical Encyclopaedia*, which must be accurate, cookery books vary to a great degree. For instance, I have had *filet de sole Portugaise* served to me in nine different ways!

Why do we use French to quote our main dishes? For many years now there has been a controversy amongst the general public and the hotel and restaurant fraternity regarding the printing of menus in English or French, and this controversy is not likely to be settled for as many years to come.

Basically the language of the kitchen is French, for we must admit that the French have done more to study the science of cooking than any other nation. The French—and possibly the Italians—are the only nations to have attempted the classification of food dishes in their infinite variety, and to have formed 'dictionaries of reference' for the proper preparation of thousands of recipes. The French have further classified their main dishes—and the variations by using names. There are not two names alike, yet each name implies a slightly different method of procedure, using slightly different ingredients in different quantities or proportions.

The average Frenchman (who, quite rightly, likes his food and its variety) understands these slight differences in names. Not so the Englishman, who is liable to become irritated by French menus. Our kitchen recipes are often based on French names just because it is impossible to translate those names into English. For example, *filet de sole Murat, filet de sole bonne femme, filet de sole Dieppoise, filet de sole Nantua, filet de sole Portugaise,* and *filet de sole Veronique* are only six ways out of several hundred of cooking a fillet of sole.

These are what we call 'classic dishes'. They are recipes produced by the famous chefs of France dating back to and during the times of Henry IV, and have been carried down through the ages. They form our 'basic kitchen'. Every cook who is worthy to be called a cook must know their ingredients and proportions, and should not deviate from the precise recipe. Unfortunately, so many of them in England just do not trouble to carry out these recipes strictly and—as I have mentioned earlier—I have had a *filet de sole Portugaise* served to me in several different ways in different establishments in England in the course of one month. The English public cannot understand this, and think that hotel menus are 'swanky'. Nothing is further from the truth. Official recipes from the grand masters, such as Brillat-Savarin, Escoffier, Vatel, and others, are dedicated recipes and must not be altered. Their mere name means something. All said and done, our recipe books are meant to be on a par with the *Pharmaceutical Encyclopaedia*, where to alter the ingredients or proportions of pills may prove fatal. Keen gardeners know that the names of flowers and plants are in Latin, not because it 'sounds better', but because each flower or plant has a variety of species stemming from the same base. The average public talks about a rose or a daffodil in the same way that they talk about a fish dish or a meat dish. They know the basic difference between sole, plaice, turbot, and halibut, or veal, beef, and mutton, but in many cases that is about all.

As in chemistry, horticulture, or atomic research, detailed rules must be laid down to get specific results.

Basic recipes in cooking are quite as important as basic recipes in other directions. A rose may be a rose, but what sort of rose— white, red, pink, yellow, polyanthus, bush, standard, half-standard?

I may parallel with: 'What sort of fish? Brown sauce, white sauce? What flavouring and garnishes?'

The above considerations are the result of the controversy about whether menus be printed in English or French, and go

F

much deeper than the public realize. Furthermore, the names are standard or should be, and in many cases are not translatable at reasonable length. We in the restaurant world have tried to put English translations on to dishes, only to make them too long in structure and too silly to read.

Take *filet de sole Veronique* and describe it in English. Your translation would read something like this, reduced to its simplest terms: 'Fillet of sole poached in its own stock with a little white wine, covered with a white sauce, garnished with white grapes and glazed (i.e. browned) in the oven.'

Try to put that on a menu card and see where it gets you! Incidentally, I have not mentioned in my *filet de sole Veronique* the basic 'white' sauce. Should it be *sauce vin blanc, sauce supreme, sauce Bechamel, sauce creme*—for they are all different basically? A second-class cook in a small establishment would most likely use a *sauce Bechamel* (literally flour and water) and forget the white wine (or drink it himself), while a good cook who knows his basic cookery books would use a *sauce vin blanc glacé*, and put the wine in the foundation of the sauce.

Thus we see the great deal of skill and knowledge that a good cook must acquire, and explains the fact why we have a five-year, full-time apprenticeship course in cooking, and even then five-year apprentice cooks can only be taught at a registered number of kitchens throughout the British Isles. For the less ambitious young man there is a three-year apprenticeship scheme in establishments of a medium order, where the best does not seem to be expected.

Thus one sees the basic reason for the use of French in cookery books: they give many thousands of recipes, all based on fundamental sauces and garnishes, but each one classified as to the minor details of flavour.

Whatever we in England may say about menus in French, the same problem arises in many other countries. The Germans, Swiss, Dutch, and Americans all use French designations to a greater or lesser degree, although their menus are written in their own language. Many a menu I have seen in Europe is a hotch-potch of languages—with French used as the key to the preparation of a dish. Two examples are: *seezunge (sole) nach Veronique art*, and *ice-cream Melba, coupe Melba, eis Melba art*. Some of these names appear to stick in the public mind. *Ice-cream*

Melba, composed by Escoffier, was a special surprise for Dame Nellie Melba on a visit to London many years ago. Everyone seems to know that it consists of vanilla ice-cream, garnished with a peach (preferably fresh), and covered with a raspberry sauce. It is often these simple dishes which catch the public taste.

Even in Spain, where all the menus are written in Spanish, key names are used. Even a *peaela*, that delightful dish composed mainly of rice and saffron, has several tags, according to the way the garnish is handled. One can have *peaela* with shellfish, *peaela* with shellfish and ordinary fish, *peaela* with chicken, chicken and shellfish, mutton and beef, fish and beef, etc. Each type of *peaela*, like cheese, has its individual name, and the public who eat in the better-class restaurants know that difference. Surely we in England should take a little more trouble to improve our knowledge in these matters. Incidentally, many hotels in Europe now print their menus in English, French, and German.

Even the Americans cannot get away entirely from the French names. They print Newburg lobster, chicken mayonnaise, pear Conde, and other names they cannot translate at reasonable length, and which have been absorbed from the French into every language. Incidentally, I do not agree with the fairly recent presentation of the American *à la carte* menu where each dish is mentioned in a complete sentence (almost a paragraph in some cases), using the most flowery, extreme, and impossible phraseology to portray its merits—even if it is only roast beef!

I suspect that this phase will work itself out in a year or so, in the same way that the American male has discarded his hundreds of extremely loud ties and reverted to the plainest of the plain neckware (1958-9).

I was well aware, when I started to write this short controversial dissertation on French cookery, that I should be laying myself open (in England at any rate) to a lot of criticism from the other school of thought who say, 'Out with French menus.' Out with 'bastard menus' (half-English, half-French), I grant you, but not entirely with French menus. Either print your menu all in English or all in French. Some of us, including my two hotels, print the luncheon menu in English and the dinner menu in French.

This has proved satisfactory, as luncheon menus lend themselves more readily to English dishes, which should be given their

English names, e.g. tripe and onions, liver and bacon, boiled silverside and dumplings, etc. Your dinner menu, on the contrary, is more liable to include sauced fish, meat, game, or poultry dishes, where the French nomenclatures become important.

My critics will have noticed that I have not yet mentioned what may—erroneously—be called British dishes. I refer, of course, to roast beef and Yorkshire pudding, saddle of mutton, boiled salmon, fried sole, steak and kidney pudding (or pie), Irish stew, Lancashire hotpot, roly-poly pudding, plum pie, fruit pies, and other well-known dishes in common use in these isles.

I have nothing whatsoever to say against these dishes, dear critics, for I eat them regularly and enjoy them thoroughly. I would point out, however, that they are all plain dishes, roasts or stews, with no intricate sauces or garnishes, and cannot be regarded as anything but what they are—plain, wholesome, well-cooked (we hope) and good.

These old English recipes in common use today have been handed down to us from generation to generation in their simple forms. And the reason for this is that the English have for centuries been known as a meat-eating nation by European peoples. Owing to our climate, we have excellent pasture-lands on which our cattle thrive. Plain roasts are therefore the obvious outcome of the opportunity afforded by good cattle, and, so far as is possible, this should be maintained.

In Europe, however, meat is, normally speaking, not so good, for indifferent pastures breed indifferent cattle. The further south one travels, the more parched the pastures and the tougher the resultant meat.

Hence through the ages we have been able to breed the best beef and mutton to feed our own people in our somewhat wet and chilly climate.

It is surely one of the laws of the universe that the hotter the climate the more cereals, fruit, vegetables and farinaceous foods are eaten by the population. Meat does not thrive because the people do not really want it as staple diet—a little matter which the Lord of the universe has attended to in a very well-balanced way.

Hence the skill of Italian, French, and Spanish cooks in preparing food of less blood-heating, calorific value, suitable to their respective countries. In fact, all one can do with meat in parts of Spain and Italy is to stew it—and stew it for a long time. One finds that in hot climates the people drink a lot of soup—they get thirsty. So what of the almost stewed-out meat? Some use must be found for it, so these more southern nations in Europe have spent much more time and thought on the preparation of what we call made-up dishes than we have had reason to do.

However, times have changed and we no longer have to rely on home-grown food—in fact, in England this is impossible, owing to the growth of the population. So that today roast beef (I do not mention Yorkshire pudding), saddle or leg of lamb or mutton, salmon, sole, and other prime foods of equal quality can be had in many parts of the world. In fact, American ribs of beef are possibly superior to ours and the French, and their mutton is equally as good.

CHAPTER SEVEN

Behind the Scenes

UP TO the advent of the really big hotel it was the correct thing for the hotel proprietor to walk round his dining-room each meal-time and talk to his guests. My amiable father was well versed in this art and always used to chat to his guests, and at the same time made sure that the food and service was correct.

Unfortunately, this 'going round the room', as we used to call it, is now lacking. It was still partially prevalent between the wars (I used to talk to guests at table up to 1946), but the courtesy has since died out with the quick-service methods of today. More is the pity, for we have lost the last link with the real 'mine host'. Now, it is the very indifferent suave or frowning head waiter who asks, 'Is everything satisfactory?' to which the guest says, 'Yes,' and the head waiter passes on. In the large establishment a restaurant manager controls and supervises that particular department. In substance he acts in lieu of a proprietor. His duties include the welcoming of guests to his dining-room in the capacity of 'mine host.'

The art of 'walking the room' in the proprietor days is quite different, and is acquired by training. It takes a little time to get used to talking to people at table, and for a shyish person like myself it can be most embarrassing. My father forced me through it, however, and indeed I am grateful that he did. The technique in the case of the proprietor is not to walk round the room and talk from table to table in sequence. Rather choose the visitors you know, and who appreciate a chat with the proprietor. In a way it makes them feel important that they are being picked out and especially recognized. During these talks (watching the service at the same time) one has a quick look-round the other occupied tables and assesses the type of people in the restaurant. Some look intrigued—hopeful that they may be recognized by the proprietor as 'worthy guests'. These guests are obviously 'approachable' and should be visited, leisurely and with a slow, natural deportment. It is unwise to approach young couples, obviously rather wrapped up in themselves, for they become embarrassed, and you—for all you know—might have interrupted a marriage proposal! The same applies to parties of business-men, whom you may interrupt in a different field—a business proposal.

All these points need studying, and after a time one gets a sense of 'atmosphere' as to whom to approach. I regret very much to say—and I reproach myself constantly—that I no longer keep up my father's training.

When I was younger—in black jacket and striped trousers, the usual hotel manager's 'uniform'—I did my duty in that way. Now that I no longer wear a black jacket and striped trousers, but in fact wear 'ordinary' dark suits, I find that I seem to embarrass people, as, owing to my age, they feel that they must stand up in my presence at their table. For my guests nervously to stand up spoils their sense of comfort, which is naturally communicated to me in a feeling of reciprocal nervousness.

Therefore, I seldom 'walk the room' these days, and on the whole I miss the friendly knowledge I had of my guests in the past.

When approaching guests, one should not always commence talking about the weather, but should endeavour to obtain a little background beforehand from the staff as to the visitors' nationality and reason for being in London, if possible (Chelsea Flower Show, Olympia, Earls Court, theatres, etc.) and talk round these points.

*

It is quite obvious that walking round the dining-room is an old custom, most probably started hundreds of years ago, when 'mine host' of the inn (in no matter which country in Europe) used to look to the welfare of his guests. That is to imply that the better innkeepers used to take this interest, for I am sure even in those days there were the lazy innkeepers who did not trouble about the guest so long as that guest paid his bill on departure.

Believe me, times have not changed in that respect, and a great many of the lazy or ignorant ones still exist among us today.

The act of 'walking the room' has a possibly more important function, however. By so doing you instantly smarten up your staff and alert that whole section of the business, from the *maître d'hotel* to the kitchen.

The general public naturally do not know the considerable organization which is involved in the running of a good restaurant, any more than I, personally, know the processes involved in the making of the pair of shoes I am wearing.

Perhaps a few details in restaurant procedure would not, therefore, come amiss.

Firstly, your restaurant and its waiters are under the control of a *maître d'hotel*, head waiter, superintendent, or restaurant manager—whichever of these titles you like to use. Anyway, he is the man responsible to the management for the smooth running of his department.

His job is not an easy one, and your good executive for this position is not easy to find. Below him are one or more assistant head waiters, who control sections of the seating accommodation, according to the size of the restaurant.

Below, again, are the station waiters—those who are responsible for the actual serving of the food ordered, and below again are the *commis de rang*, or junior assistant waiters, whose job it is to collect the dirty plates and bring ordered dishes from the kitchen to the station waiter, who serves the food to the customer. The juniors should wear white bow-ties and the head waiters black bow-ties, as a sign of authority. (Unfortunately, one sees slack hotel managers allowing junior waiters to wear black bow-ties in certain establishments—a matter for regret.)

Your head waiter books tables and keeps a table plan for each meal. He also directs you to your table on arrival, or, if he is occupied, delegates an assistant head waiter to do this for him.

The head waiter or second head waiter sees you seated and produces the menu, from which you order your meal. He is conversant with the dishes and can advise you accordingly. He then enters your order on a kitchen requisition pad in triplicate, which he hands to an assistant waiter, who leaves one copy on the station service table, gives one to the kitchen, and the other copy to the restaurant cashier for entry on the final bill.

Not only must the head waiter take the order correctly, he must apply good handwriting too, or the kitchen will do a little swearing on a point of illegibility; and the service may get held up or the wrong dish supplied. Faced with these alternatives, the head waiter—and in fact all waiters—quickly acquire good handwriting.

The order then passes to the station waiter, who is responsible for from four to five tables, each with from two to four guests normally. He has to serve each individual dish in some sort of rotation, so that he does not give too quick attention to one table and too slow attention to another. Your station waiter never knows when his tables will become occupied, but he must nevertheless keep things running smoothly. He relies partly on his assistant waiter to achieve this, for once the table order is on the station serving table, the assistant has to keep his 'chef' fed with the dishes as they are required, course by course.

Before each dish is served, the assistant waiter puts a clean plate before the guest, and after each course he takes away the dirty plates and silver.

As there may be fifteen people seated at five tables, all with different orders and at different stages in a meal, one can willingly realize the amount of organization, quick and accurate thinking, and timing which a good station 'team' must possess to give efficient service to its customers.

Slow service, when it occurs, is often due to a mistaken order or some hold-up in the kitchen, such as a special dish which must be given sufficient time to cook—a point which so many guests fail to understand. Table waiters do not like to take drink orders, for it puts them out of their stride, so a wine waiter is generally available, whose sole duty it is to look after guests' needs in this direction.

So you see, during meal hours your waiter is fully occupied. We often receive complaints of so-called 'indifferent attention' from waiters. These complaints are generally from the type of non-understanding guest who expects the first waiter in sight to serve him. This type of guest does not realize that because a waiter passes his table he is not necessarily there to serve him, but is busily engaged in a journey to the kitchen about an order for another station waiter. It is very riling for a guest to see several waiters standing at a service table, apparently doing nothing, and not to receive any attention. This should not really happen, but here again the waiter in charge of that visitor may well be in the kitchen actually obtaining the dish which the guest has ordered. The apparently 'idle' waiters belong to other stations, but I agree that they should at least go to the guest and explain.

Waiters do not only serve at meals; they have the responsibility of laying-up the tables, changing the table-cloths, seeing their plates and silver are sent up to them clean, attending to the cruets, glasses, and water-jugs, and have to vacuum the carpet and dust the chairs. Soiled linen, after each meal, must be taken down to the linen-room, counted, and replaced with clean.

So that, even without touching on the kitchen procedure, you note that there is a lot of organization required to run a restaurant. A terrific amount of personality must be used, for the human element is always uppermost—a human element from many countries with many languages, with which your head waiter has to deal and co-ordinate.

Help-yourself service has come to stay, I am afraid, but, please, never in a really good restaurant.

Kitchen

You are now meeting the men who make your hotel a home from home. Come with me and see them at work: observe how exacting their task is. Much has been written in and out of fiction concerning the chef, who, it appears, spends his time ramping and raving and throwing stew-pans about.

Does he? His calling demands as much knowledge and con-centration as does that of the chief in a chemical laboratory. In a big kitchen the various sections are as follows:

1. *Chef.* Supervises the preparation and service of the food from the kitchen to all the dining-rooms. Ensures econ-omy. Arranges the menus. Tastes the food for correct seasoning. Plans the cooking times for completion before dining-room service begins. Checks that the food is garnished properly. Gives all the dishes a final inspection before service.

2. *Sauce-cook.* Makes soups and sauces for the various dishes. Roasts and grills meat and poultry if no roast cook is available.

3. *Vegetable-cook.* Assists the sauce-cook and cooks all the vegetables.
4. *Roast-cook.* Roasts and grills meat and poultry.
5. *Fish-cook.* Prepares all fish dishes and, very often, egg dishes as well.
6. *Larder-cook* (usually called *garde manger*). Is in charge of the preparation of all cold foods—that is, *hors d'œuvre*, cold meats, canapes, sandwiches, all mayonnaise dressing, meats and salads.
7. *Pastry-cook.* Prepares all pastry, desserts, cakes, jellies, sweets, and ices.
8. *Butcher.* Prepares all meats, fish, and poultry. (Often works with the *garde manger*.)
9. *Breakfast-cook.* On early duty. Cooks all breakfast dishes.
10. *Stillroom Staff.* Prepares tea, coffee, cocoa, hot milk, and suchlike things. Makes toast (breakfast), and Melba toast (lunch). Cuts bread and butter and sandwiches for afternoon tea.
11. *Staff-cook.* Cooks meals for the staff.
12. *Kitchen Porter.* Clean vegetables, washes plates, silver, pots, and pans, and keeps the kitchen clean.

In a really big hotel each of these cooks may have one or more assistants, according to the size of the establishment. A large number of kitchens, however, do not have all these sections; one cook combines the duties of two or more. Others, however, have a greater number: for instance, Grosvenor House, the Dorchester, the Savoy, the Connaught Rooms, and others, each have as many as 100 cooks employed at one time. This total is divided amongst several kitchens, for here again centralization can be overdone and bottle-necks created. The bigger establishments generally organize their cooking into specialist kitchens: one for the restaurant, one for the grill, one for banqueting, and sometimes—but not usually—one for floor service in bedrooms and suites. The Grosvenor House—or the Savoy with 1,000 employees—also has a special kitchen for staff meals.

Let us come back to the Goring Hotel, with its 100 rooms and its good restaurant business. Here we have twelve cooks, one on each section (sauce, fish, roast, cold-room, vegetables, pastry, *entremetier*, breakfast), three apprentices, and the Chef.

The speed and variety of kitchen work today makes these numbers imperative, for each department may have as many as fifteen to twenty different orders being prepared at one time. Hence a cook not only has to be a good cook, but he has to have a quiet mind and a retentive memory while he is doing his cooking.

To go into a kitchen as a layman during 'service' is bedlam. You will hear the chef or an *aboyer* (shouter) (sometimes described as 'the kitchen clerk') standing in front at the service-table hot-plate, calling out the orders as the waiters bring them in from the restaurant.

Each order is written on a check by the waiter, who hands the check to the *aboyer*, who shouts the order and then files the check on a series of spikes until the order is fulfilled. This alone takes great concentration on the part of the chef, for each check often contains the order for a whole meal, and each course must be dished up and served in rotation. With anything up to 100 different orders going at the same time one can imagine the acute and nervous tension through which a chef works twice a day. The waiter stands and waits, but says nothing. On the other hand, each cook must 'accept' (verbally acknowledge) each order.

The language is invariably kitchen French, the use of which we have already discussed in its relation to the menu: now and then a distraught apprentice cook lapses into English. It is the half-understood and the misunderstood kitchen scene that has influenced so much bad fiction. Here are kitchen facts. The next time I meet a chef in a novel, I hope the author will have learned a little of the intense concentration required. It goes something like this:

'*Ca Marche—deux lunch—deux œufs du jour—deux.*'
'*Oui.*'
'*Et deux roast beef—deux.*'
'*Oui.*'
'*Deux pommes et legumes—deux.*'
'*Oui.*'
'*Patissier—un flan aux cerises.*'
'*Entendu.*'
'*Ca Marche—trois lunch—deux spaghetti, un œuf du jour.*'
'*Oui.*'
'*Et deux goulash—deux—un poisson du jour—un.*'

'Oui'—'Oui' (two sections involved here—sauce- and fish-cooks).

'*Les quatorze menu à la carte.*'

'*Les quatorze passe à table fait envoyer—les quatorze crème longchamps—quatorze.*'

'*Oui.*'

'*Saucier—en dix minutes quatorze filet de sole bonne femme—quatorze.*'

'*Oui.*'

'*Grill—un quart-d'heure-quatorze tournedos, dix au point, quatre au bleu—quatorze.*'

'*Oui.*'

'*Patissier—les quatorze sont à tables faites marcher les souffle vanille vingt-cinq minutes.*'

'*Entendu.*'

'*Ca Marche—deux lunch. Garde manger—neuf huitres—neuf—sitot prets.*'

'*Oui.*'

'*A suivre—grill deux lamb chop—deux au point.*'

'*Oui.*'

'*Garde Manger, les hors d'œuvres manque la haut—supplement de suite.*'

'*Oui.*'

And so it goes on from 12.30 to 2.30 at lunch-time and 6.30 onwards at dinner-time.

In addition to his knowledge and skill, the chef must have organizing ability—*mise en place*—the putting into place. Apart from the breakfast-cook, work begins at 9 a.m., giving the chef two hours to prepare his dishes for the menu of the day—goulash, *vol-au-vent*, beef for roasting, leg of lamb for roasting, potatoes peeled, vegetables washed and cut into portions, eggs boiled hard, base sauces checked, stock-pot replenished, consommé clarified, thick soup prepared, fish gutted, and a hundred other things. For this, in a big kitchen, each section cook will have one or two assistants, or *commis* cooks, according to the amount of work to be handled in each sector. Again, others have none and work single-handed. All this takes place in the main kitchen.

The side kitchens—namely, the larder (*garde manger*) and the pastry—have their own jobs. The cook of the former prepares and bones any meat or game, or trusses chickens, ready to hand to the stove cooks in the quantities ordered by the chef. He then turns to his *hors d'œvres* or similar cold dishes.

The pastry-cook prepares various pastry crusts, makes pastries and flans (open tarts), prepares fruit salad, makes cake mixtures, jellies and trifles. This department is quite as hard-worked as the main kitchen, but can take things more leisurely, for it is not harrowed by the terrific rush of stove-work when things liven up during meal hours. The larder and the pastry departments are always kept separate but near the main kitchen, partly because of the heat factor, but largely because of the quieter attitude of mind required.

Many hotels have not enough work for a full-time larder-man, and when this is the case the chef personally does his butchering in the morning for the whole day. This is often the best plan, for a chef who is a good butcher can certainly get more portions out of a piece of meat than an indifferent larder-cook, who sometimes cuts to waste.

The reader will begin to feel that I am biased in favour of chefs, that I am 'covering up' the tantrums and temper for which they are notorious, but I am not; the argument of a flung frying-pan can occasionally be used. I should know, having myself been on the receiving end! The chef carries a heavy responsibility: the reputation of the house depends largely on him. Cooking is hot work, and must be carried out to an exact time-table to be ready at the right time of day. It must be so organized that meat, fish, eggs, vegetables, puddings, and pies are ready at the same time. Dishes cannot be 'held' too long or the sauces will 'break', the soup will burn, the roast dry. One of the most common failings in a cook is the use of too much salt, for a cook—always with the smell of food in his nostrils—is inclined to over-season dishes. That is why a conscientious chef walks round his stove just before lunch and checks up on the work of his brigade. He still has time to correct faults if they are not too bad. For instance, he finds his soup too salty: well, there might be time to put some potatoes to boil in with it in order to draw off the salt. That is but one of the tricks of the trade, a matter to be expected: the chef does not necessarily go mad and bite people because of little things like that.

It is when a hopeless idiot persistently does something wrong during the service of meals that a chef is sometimes driven to the flung-frying-pan technique. I find it better to walk away on such occasions. It is unwise to correct a chef in a temper; he loses face with his subordinates. Cooks are temperamental, but cooks understand cooks, and the chef engages his own staff in a large establishment. After all, he knows what he wants if he is a good chef, and he has to work with them, anyhow.

A chef's rhetoric when he is upset can be quite picturesque. We once had a pastry-cook who would have won no medals in a confectionery exhibition. One day my wife went down to speak to him about something, and as she approached the pastry larder she saw the Chef enter before her. He stood with his back towards her, oblivious of her presence, and proceeded to 'tear a strip off' the poor man—it is a pity that for printability's sake I must purge it of its piquant profanity. The pastry-cook had no kitchen French, hence Chef was compelled to express himself in ripe—over-ripe—kitchen English:

'You dirty, rotten, stinking, idiot pig! You make me for to stamp my feet on your ceiling-plaster mixture you call it icing— to jump upon your cement and sand with stones in—your what you call it a cake to make a tank-traps. You feeble-minded, elephant-fisted son of an unmarried mother and a father from the jail. Such a thing you call it a cake I would not see fit to use it to poison a mangy dog, or some policeman he pinch me for cruelty to dumb animals. You mixer-up of concrete. You stinking-muck swine. You worm in the interior part of a consumptive monkey. You . . .'

Just then the *commis*, who had come into range, saw my wife and dropped a warning wink to the Chef, but he, poor man, being quite beside himself, interpreted it as an act of insolence and broadened his horizon to include seven generations of the *commis's* ancestors and five of his future progeny. The youth, however, nothing daunted, proved himself a diplomat.

'Can I help you, madam?' he asked.

Chef swivelled round. His jaw dropped on to his chest and, with a murmured apology, he departed.

This was the first time my wife had tasted high tension in the kitchen, but it was, in fact, nothing very much out of the way: the cake was not so bad but that it might have been much worse, and then so would have been Chef's language. Cooks take a 'telling-off' of this kind in their stride, but I can't see the manager of a factory getting away with it: the works would be at a standstill while the shop steward mounted the soap-box.

It is not because all cooks are foreigners full of Latin temperament and all factory workers Englishmen stolidly Anglo-Saxon. It is because cooking is a passion—a compulsion—and cooks, like artists or writers, will sacrifice security and comfort in order to cook.

The average Englishman believes that cookery is a feminine accomplishment—that men can engage in it only on naval or merchant ships and in military camps where large-scale destruction of good food by fire, heat, smoke, and water is accepted as cooking. The idea is erroneous. The average woman does household cooking better than the average man does it, but a good male cook is superior to a woman in a large-scale kitchen. Further, it is not foreigners only who have the urge to cook, and when an English boy has that goal in sight nothing will keep him out of the kitchen. If his parents object, he will leave home and enter cooking by way of the kitchen porter's tasks, notwithstanding that had he abandoned his ambition he would have been 'sitting pretty' in his father's office knowing that one day he would inherit an entirely different business.

Having the flair for a calling is not enough: even an artist has to study art, and the cook has before him years of hard work and intensive study. Apprentices—who can be accepted only in the best selected and listed hotels—have a five-year contract. After that all-round experience, they generally specialize on one part of the stove or another: we find that some prefer preparing sauces, others like to roast, others, again, go in for fish-cooking. There was a time when pastry-cooks could do general cooking also, but those days are past, and now our pastry-cooks, who do not simply make pie-crust and pastry, obtain their training as confectioners.

The cycle of a first-class cook is in three stages. He starts as an apprentice at about sixteen years of age for all-round training. By twenty-one he is free of indentures and will take a position in any of the seven sections of a big kitchen, and, at a mature age, may become a *chef de cuisine* with a four-figure salary. The longest landing on the climb to this eminence is the position of second-in-command.

To reach this status, a cook must pass through all sections (or *parties*, as we call them in the kitchen) until he becomes sauce-cook or *saucier*. He then is No. 2, and takes command when the chef is absent.

Another important post in the kitchen is that of *tournant*—he is proficient in every *partie*, and he takes charge when the regular cook in each department has his day off. The hotel is alive for twenty-four hours a day and is active seven days a week. Each member of the staff has his day of rest, but not always on Sunday. For each member of the team who is absent on his day off, there must be a substitute. It is not only time and tide that wait for no man, but it is temperature and the tummy! The former has to be kept as near constant as possible, so someone stokes the boilers when the regular stoker is away; the latter insists on being filled, and the kitchen caters. The chef carries the responsibility whether he is 'on' or 'off'.

He must be a good cook himself, and be able to correct mistakes. He must be a disciplinarian, yet able to keep the loyalty and affection of his team. He must be able to judge a good cook when he engages one, in order not to have to make too many changes in, at least, his head men. He must set a standard in his kitchen, and know how to keep it up. He must know his quantities, for he is usually responsible for the buying of fresh provisions (meat, fish, vegetables) daily, and he must show the percentage of profit each month as decided by the hotel control. In other words, he is a man who is the master-mind in his department.

The manager may be the man on the navigation bridge, but the chef is the chief engineer: they make a point of meeting each other every morning to discuss programmes—functions, changes in the menu, and the like.

A good *saucier* does not necessarily make a good chef. Often the contrary is the case. A cook, notwithstanding his knowledge and first-class workmanship, often lacks the type of mind that can worry about percentage profits, control, organizing, and engaging staff.

Whilst most of them know their buying, and the amounts to use, they are too nervous to take full responsibility. I have often noticed this—in fact, most of my ex-sauce-cooks, (and I keep them for about four years on the average) have broken down when left in charge during the chef's holidays.

The kitchen loses that decisive tone of the master-mind, and one sees the staff there gradually slacking off through want of that little stiffening. The food may remain of the same quality and flavour and percentages may be all right, but by the end of the first fortnight the pep has gone from the kitchen. The visitor notices nothing, he may even say that the food is better, but we feel in our blood that things are running down. Many of my *sauciers* have left to take jobs as chef, but generally I advise them to go to smaller or country hotels at first, until they feel their capacity for control.

They find that to succeed they must work more with the management and less with their cooks. Under these conditions it is better for them to change their position and come into a new place as a chef, so that their background will not be known to their fellow workers. It is not only better for the promoted cook; it is better for the establishment. Often have friends said to me, 'My old chef retired, and I put in my *saucier*, who has been with me for six years, but——' I know exactly what a ramification of dissatisfaction that 'but' implies.

Experience has taught me that if the manager or proprietor does not know his kitchen, he will never have a good chef. He may engage one, but as soon as that chef discovers that his manager has but a vague conception of the kitchen, the standard will fall. Cooks like to be appreciated, in the same way that a good pianist plays to his audience. When the chef knows that you know what you want, and how to get a standard and keep it, he will co-operate willingly and look up to you. Unfortunately, so many hotel managers of today have never been through a kitchen—or have at the most spent six months in it. These are the all too frequent types of managers who say to the chef, 'I leave it to you, Chef.' No suggestion of special menus, no costing, discussions of ingredients required—just 'I leave it to you, Chef—your department!' I have seen this happen often. A good chef takes a new job and is discouraged by a clueless manager. On the contrary, I have also seen a not-too-good chef improve considerably under the right manager. We all like to have someone to advise us at times, and a chef is no exception.

Housekeeping

Is it felt that I harp too much on the kitchen? It is impossible to do that. I am not so unappreciative of other behind-the-scene workers!

For example, the housekeeper in her sphere is as important as the chef is in his. My father used to say: 'We make profit while our guests sleep, so see that they sleep in peace.'

That peaceful repose is provided via the housekeeper. She is not, of course, guardian of a guest's conscience, but she is guardian of his comfort, so even those who suffer from insomnia for internal reasons can spend their sleepless nights in uncramped repose.

The housekeeping department is an essentially feminine occupation, although, strange to say, I have written the standard text-book on the subject for our Hotel and Catering Institute, which is read in all our technical colleges and taught to would-be housekeepers. Hotel cooking is not domestic cooking magnified, but hotel housekeeping is home housewifery on a large scale. There are slovenly housewives who do not get divorced and there are incompetent hotel housekeepers who do not get dismissed.

Housekeepers very rarely start as chambermaids and 'work up'. They are generally young ladies with a flair for the work, and until recently they learned their job by acting as hotel assistants, giving an all-round hand in several departments, until they became assistant housekeepers. There they remained until the age of thirty or more before being appointed head if more than one is kept. A head housekeeper must have a strong personality to be able to correct, organize and control her staff of not only chambermaids and house-porters, but daily cleaners, morning charwomen, linen staff (of whom she is nominally in charge, but with whom she seldom interferes), and in fact all female staff. She must have a pleasing presence herself and see that her chambermaids follow her example, in speech as well as in habits of cleanliness. She is directly responsible to the manager. Her daily routine calls for long hours, from 7 a.m. at the latest to 10 p.m. at the earliest, with time off in the afternoon. She is liable to be called in the night, for example, in the case of the illness of a lady guest. She is responsible for the cleanliness of the hotel, as well as discipline in her bedrooms. A really good single-handed housekeeper can handle up to seventy bedrooms, but after that she will need an assistant. This makes her hours much less arduous, because she can arrange her duties to better advantage.

At the Goring we have two housekeepers, both of whom lead a strenuous life, but obviously enjoy their work. Early duty entails controlling charwomen in the hall, seeing the maids are on their floors by 7 a.m. and that they start sweeping and vacuuming the corridors, serving early morning tea to visitors, and attending to other wants.

A list of guests departing and of others arriving is then collected from the reception office, and the information is passed to the chambermaids in all sections, so that the necessary linen can be changed in the required manner. The inspection of rooms, both empty and occupied, is the afternoon work of the housekeeper on duty. Beds must be checked for proper making (mitreing corners of sheets and other technical points), cleanliness of carpets and upholstery looked to, basins and baths inspected, tiles in bathrooms scrutinized, lavatory pans examined, toilet rolls checked, and, most important, she should run her finger along any ridges for dust! While this inspection is taking place, defects should be noted, such as a broken glass table-top, dripping taps, loose screws, squeaky beds, burnt-out light bulbs and other little things. These should be noted in a duplicate book and the top copy be handed to the maintenance department at once. Rectification of faults on the same day is the ideal.

An occasional inspection with the manager should be made in order to discuss the major problems outside her direct control, such as the condition of carpets, the need for entire redecoration, or for only a wash-down by painters, new wallpaper, a change in colour of curtains and upholstery, and other home-like items. This, in turn, is generally referred to the higher authority of the proprietor or to a member of the board of directors acquainted with the financial position and policy of the hotel.

Apart from these duties, the housekeeper is responsible for the changing of net curtains throughout the whole hotel—no minor job in London. These are generally done floor by floor, or section by section, according to the size of the establishment. The changing of eiderdowns and cushions is the housekeeper's department, too, and she must have a reserve store for the purpose.

At the Goring Hotel we wash our own net curtains in an electric machine, and shampoo our own carpets and chairs. We also make our own heavy curtains. Here again the housekeeper and my wife supervise a special staff of four who are employed full-time on this work. The Goring Hotel has always been known as one of the best-kept and cleanest hotels in London. I am not writing this boastingly—it is a fact recognized by our thousands of visitors. This very high standard was created by my mother (herself an hotel housekeeper before her marriage), who from 1910 until 1914 looked after things herself, with the help of an assistant.

From 1914 to 1916 a Miss Smith was housekeeper, and when the hotel was commandeered Miss Smith went as head house-keeper to Claridge's Hotel, where she remained for several years until her retirement.

After 1918, on reopening, an executive staff was very difficult to find and the hotel suffered from some appalling specimens. When I took over in 1924, however, a Miss Wilkins was firmly installed, and remained our head housekeeper until after the war in 1946. She was then well over retiring age and stayed only to please me—for she hated the bombing. I owe her a great debt of gratitude.

After the war we had some shocking housekeepers. One I turfed out overnight after she had been with us but a few weeks. I learned that she was endeavouring to 'procure' chambermaids. Another one, with a very good reference from a large London hotel, started to have the bedroom heavy curtains remade by turning them inside out. She went.

Then came Mrs. Hersee, the widow of an hotel manager who had successfully operated the best hotel in Basra. I am sure she is remembered by many of our present-day visitors, for she made a point of being as friendly as possible and looking after their little personal needs (extra pillow, no bolster, extra chair, odds and ends of personal preference). She rejuvenated the personal service book, as we call it, detailing special requests. To be greeted and known—even by your particular little 'wants'—is good hotel-keeping.

After about seven years Mrs. Hersee retired in order to keep house for her son. She was succeeded by Mrs. Schoeffter (of English nationality), who had been second housekeeper for some two years. Her entry into hotel housekeeping bears out my first point concerning adaptability. She had lived in Belgium for some years, knew nothing about the hotel business, and frankly said so when she applied for the post of second housekeeper.

I could see her personality, but, as I was in no hurry, I did not engage her. Still not suited after another fortnight, I asked her to call again and 'gave her a trial'. She fell into the routine easily, and she keeps the house in spotless condition, as well as attending to the curtains and the workroom, which is a comparatively new venture, and did not operate during Mrs. Hersee's time.

Hotel bedrooms are often checked by symbols. In a well-organized house, the plug chains will be placed over the taps. This is not strictly for tidiness, although it looks neat: it is to tell the housekeeper on inspection that the bath or basin has been cleaned (in the chambermaids' viewpoint). If the chain is not over the tap, it implies that the maid is coming back and the room is not yet completely ready.

I teach my housekeepers to watch for chambermaids' kinks. If I find something wrong in one room, I at once look for the same fault in other rooms which are in the charge of the same maid. Every maid—or nearly every maid—has a blind spot. One will never polish the mirrors, another will not clean the toothglasses, a third leaves dust on ledges, a fourth does not clean out drawers thoroughly, and a fifth has some other curious lack. A good housekeeper soon gets to know the failings of each maid, and it is comparatively simple to check these faults by constant reminders.

CHAPTER EIGHT

Staff

ONE of the secrets of successful hotel-keeping is to be able to pick the right type of staff and, having picked them, to keep them.

The Goring has a very good record in this respect, for forty per cent. of the employees have been in the hotel's service for from five years up to twenty-five years and more.

How often have I heard remarks from visitors to the effect that 'a certain hotel may be all right—but they cannot keep their staff'. This is sometimes the fault of the management, and sometimes the circumstance of seasonal hotel employment.

Again, in factory or industrial life, the employee is only a unit —good or bad—seen by no one of the general public. He comes, and goes, under trade rules, and his place in the factory concerned is filled by another. He tries to stay in one job with one firm only because he has his house or home nearby. He may be very skilful at his job, but his personality is of little importance to the company for whom he works. His job is to be a skilled, intelligent work-man.

Personality is essential in many hotel departments, and this puts the hotel industry on a different basis from other industries.

Thus, I repeat, one of the secrets of successful hotel-keeping is to be able to pick the right type of staff—and to keep them. If the staff have pride in their work and confidence in the good standing and capability of the management to maintain their status—and livelihood—they will remain in the one position for many, many years, and enjoy their duty periods as well as their off-duty periods.

Up to 1939 I was my father's Manager at the Goring Hotel, a position I had occupied since 1924, at a very small salary. For that period of fifteen years I controlled the hotel under my father's supervision. During those years I did my own typing, answering correspondence, taking stock sheet returns every month, including staff control, room-inspection, cellar control and issues, and kitchen control, etc.

Being of a certain age and married by then, I suggested to my father that my duties were becoming somewhat onerous, especially in view of the prosperity of the Goring Hotel and the vastly increased turnover. So I engaged a Mr. W. N. Pennington as my immediate assistant, to take over the day-to-day control and thus relieve me of certain duties and responsibilities.

Mr. Pennington joined the staff in March 1939. Before the end of the year, however, he had joined up for the war. On his return after the war, Mr. Pennington relieved me of a further considerable amount of day-to-day routine work. As the business increased, so his obligations increased and by 1946 he already had an Assistant Manager in the form of a young trainee trying to make the difficult grade to good managementship. These young men—engaged for one year only at a time, gained great knowledge and experience on the executive side of hotel keeping.

Thus over ten years I have had ten Assistant Managers under Mr. Pennington. Apart from two who were killed in motor-crashes (of course, the best two I ever had), the other eight are now well settled in good positions. Several have been abroad, and one returned from the Bahamas, where he had been in charge of a very prosperous concern for two years. As so often happens, his wife's health suffered and he had to return to England.

Now, as the business continues to increase, a permanent Assistant Manager has taken charge of such matters as banqueting, staff control, wedding receptions, cellars, and other duties delegated to him.

The oldest member of my staff—in terms of service—but still a young man, is F. Scott, who joined the staff as a young valet in 1928, and for the last year or so has been promoted to second hall porter.

The second oldest inhabitant—also still a young man under fifty—is his opposite number, W. M. Goodenough—universally known as Mersh. Scott and Mersh were in charge of the fourth-floor valet and luggage service for a term of twenty years, and are known to thousands of our guests. Mersh also joined the staff in 1928—as basement porter. He was quickly promoted to window-cleaner/floor porter, and was made a valet when about twenty-five years of age. Both these men were absent during the war on active service.

Arthur Griffiths joined the staff in 1929 and was for many years head night porter until he was called up in 1939, when he was attached to the Corps of Signals in radar services. He returned in 1945 and was promoted to head hall porter. Unfortunately, his health broke down last year. Griffiths, again, was known to thousands of our guests.

'Little' Andrews—he still looks a boy, although he does not always necessarily act like one—started in as a junior floor waiter in 1932. During the war he was posted to Canada for air-crew training, but returned to his old job as soon as he could. For nine years previous to the war he acted as second floor waiter to a floor head waiter of the name of Virtue, thus making a team which many of our regular guests knew well.

So we train our staff in order that a senior vacancy can be filled by a man of long service who is due for upgrading, and knows not only the hotel, but also its guests.

Nicol, now head hall porter, joined the hotel in 1933 and was second in the hall for many years, apart from his military service during the war.

Unseen, and unknown to any visitor, and right at the other end of the scale is W. Burley—known below stairs as 'Wally'—who has been washing plates single-handed regularly since 1933. He is far more efficient than any dish-washing machine, and at a rough guess I reckon he has washed 1,500 plates (minimum) per day during his period of service. Mathematics show that 1,500 plates a day is 9,000 per six-day week, or 450,000 per year, making a grand total of about 13,000,000 plates. He would be surprised if I gave him this figure. Apart from these duties he is also in charge of the floor service lifts.

Wally has a 'tongue' which can be heard from his basement food-service lifts to the waiters in the third floor room service department. He does not need his 'tongue' for there is an adequate telephone service from his basement position to the waiters' floor service. However, as this floor service is not within sight, he automatically feels that he must shout. His 'tongue' is getting better after twenty-five years' service, but the fact remains that it can still be heard through outside windows as well as by the normal and usually quicker telephone. I doubt if Wally has ever even been up to the third-floor room service which he keeps so adequately supplied.

Unfit for war service, Wally literally lived in the hotel. During the air-raid nights throughout the war he slept for weeks at a stretch on the kitchen floor, and he has never had a day off for sickness.

Our head of the painting and decorating staff, H. J. Powell, came to me in 1934. For some time previously he had worked as foreman for the firm who undertook our annual painting programme. On starting my own repairs and decorations department, however, I was lucky enough to secure Powell's services, and put him in charge. Before the last war—about 1936— Powell had a very bad operation for pleurisy. He was in hospital for months. When he was released he came back to me, saying that he would never have another illness as long as he lived. This proved correct. For the last twenty years he had not had a day off duty for illness, although, when over seventy years of age, he often worked half-days only. Unfortunately, he died quite suddenly early in 1960.

Powell was one of the old sort who could mix his own paints with hardly ever a mistake. Today one buys 'ready-stained' paints off a colour chart. All the big firms do it, but none of them state how the resultant colour has been blended. One can take three blended stained paints of the same colour. All these paints are liable to 'fly' in a different colour direction six months after application according to their basic colour blend. As an example, one of the worst (but unfortunately the most popular) 'stainers' is chrome—which goes to 'butter colour' very quickly. Brunswick red, on the other hand, brought up to the same paint shade to commence with, shades to a much clearer colour after six months. The same applies to greens: use blues rather than chromes in mixing in this case. We have found it almost impossible to 'pass' a shade of paint in a room unless we know its texture. It is not what it looks like on being applied: it is the colour it will fade to up (or down) after six months.

Unfortunately, the old craftsman painter is dying out. Now

the so-called painter slaps stuff on the wall which is provided by a firm off a 'colour chart'. Even foreman painters today are often not able to add stainers to white paint, due to sheer ignorance.

Incidentally, Powell had a very industrious wife, and I am sure I am letting out a secret when I say that all the lace chair arms and antimacassars in the lounge were knitted by Mrs. Powell. Good teamwork in an hotel is always appreciated. I have maintained throughout my business life that a good craftsman is worth consideration. What better way then than by helping the craftsman's wife, or family, to earn a supplementary living if their talents permit.

This reminds me that before the war I had a 'brotherhood' of Welsh boys from a very hard-working and worthwhile family. The 'Sheehan brothers' started in employment when employment in the coal-mines was at a very low ebb in about 1926. The senior Sheehan became head floor waiter in 1928. We then had a succession of Sheehan's—until we reached a total of five. Two were young waiters, one was a first-class telephone operator, and another was a hall attendant. All of them good men in their own particular department. Those were the days of Welsh colliery troubles and the General Strike.

The entire Sheehan family left at the outbreak of war in 1939 and I have not heard of them since.

My kitchen chef, M. Paul Gasc (there is only one 'chef' in a kitchen, as the word implies), has been with me since 1937.

I chose him at that time for his great experience in control positions. I found he had been a *commis* cook at the Carlton Hotel, London, under the great Escoffier, at the beginning of the century. Unfortunately, in those days, this 'honourable employment' was worth about 12s. per week. M. Gasc did not stay too long— Escoffier or no Escoffier.

At that time Escoffier, although a master cook, was not known as the chef who would eventually produce his famous *Escoffier Encyclopaedia* of cooking recipes. Incidentally, these recipes were written in collaboration with other people.

Gasc followed his career with ten years as *saucier* (head cook) at the Ritz Hotel in London. He then had two years as *sous-chef* at Quaglino's, followed by two years as *sous-chef* at the Savoy Hotel Restaurant.

Like all first-class master chefs, Gasc has a temper. The

atmosphere in a big kitchen is always hot, whether one works in Spain, France, Switzerland, Italy, Germany, America, or Iceland.

'Jock' Grant, a Scotsman, joined the staff as a valet in July 1939, after eight years' service at Selsdon Park Hotel. He became a godsend to me. Suffering from defective eyesight, he was not liable to military service, and soon after the war started he became my head (and often only) night porter. Many are the nights we spent on duty together during air raids, and many are the stories he could tell about conditions of the general public—and serving men of all nations—with whom he had to deal.

The war over, he returned to his position as valet. He is still with me, a married man with a married daughter who is quite an organist. He himself has a very useful voice, which brings him in the odd money at good-class concerts. Jock, who lives about twelve miles from Victoria Station (twenty-five minutes by train), only let me down once during the war. The railway was blocked by bomb damage, and so trains were not running. Jock Grant took a private car—at considerable expense—and arrived on night duty only one hour late. He knew that, had he failed to appear, I personally would have been landed with night duty, which entails lighting the main boilers and kitchen fires, apart from answering the telephone, cleaning the lounges, and getting the early morning teas and breakfasts ready!

Our head waiter, Toni (Perilli) came to me at the beginning of the war. Actually, he left the Claridge's Causerie when it shut down in November 1939. For some reason or other, he was 'commandeered' for factory service and for several years spent his time watching lathes: the square peg in the round hole!

Toni is a good staff-organizer. He is strict, yet reasonable—a very necessary qualification in view of the ten to twelve European junior staff, with little knowledge of English, I always employ as assistant waiters. These young men come to England on exchange permits, which allow them to work for one year at one establishment in order to learn English and to see how our hotel system works. In exchange we try to send a corresponding number of young English waiters to Europe to learn French, German, and Spanish. Toni definitely runs one of the best restaurant brigades in London for politeness, polish, and good service.

W. A. Byrne, that saturnine, dark, second head waiter, whose work now lies chiefly as banqueting and Ebury Room head waiter, also came to the hotel in 1939 (September). He occupied a position as station waiter for many years before being made official second head waiter only a few years ago. During the war he was in the Forces, engaged on radar-operation.

Have a talk to Byrne at some time. He is one of the most interesting conversational head waiters I have met. He keeps himself up-to-date with his visitors, has a very good memory, and can converse with his guests on subjects well away from the hotel industry.

*

Thus passes the pre-war period. During the war we had to put up with a number of wasters and rotters, who were only kept under control by the loyalty of the few remaining regular staff. Many a tale I could tell about their inefficiency, and I would class them today as quite unemployable, if they are still alive.

The war over, however, a new and good type of person applied for employment.

From my records, ten people who started their employment here during 1946-8 are still in active service. These include valets (1), maintenance (1), chambermaids (4), waiters (1), linen-room, etc. (2), telephone (1).

Boots

In the olden days the word 'boots' was used for a man who normally cleaned the footwear of the guests of an hotel or inn. I mention the word 'inn' on purpose, for an inn was frequented by travellers either on horseback or by coach. The roads were bad and extremely dirty, with the result that travellers arrived (riding or otherwise) with boots which really had to be cleaned. Today such dirty boots are not the normal task of a member of an hotel staff. Horses and coaches have given way to motor cars, and roads are no longer covered with white (or brown) mud, sometimes inches thick.

Today one arrives in any city in the world with reasonably clean shoes (not boots) and expects them to be merely 'wiped over' by the hotel (erstwhile inn) staff.

Dubbin, paraffin, wax, and other heavy waterproofing agents are no longer used in shoe-cleaning. Just a light shine—on an almost already existing shine—is needed. Every hotel guest has noticed that his room number is often chalked on the sole of his shoes in a position where it is hoped he will not see it. This means that the porter cleaning the shoes knows from which room (or from outside which door) they have come, and thus a check on room identity is established. It is so easy to make a mistake over shoes. We all buy our shoes as we need them, but it is astonishing how many shoes are alike in size, shape, and toe-cap markings. Only a year ago we, at the Goring Hotel, had a complaint from a visitor who had returned to Canada, stating that he had found an 'odd' pair of shoes which he had packed in his luggage before leaving London. He claimed a new pair from the hotel—quite unreasonably, in my opinion, as no one had any proof of his exact movements in other hotels. A similar case occurred only this year, when a gentleman claimed a new pair of shoes for a pair of his that had 'got mixed up'. He admitted the shoes replaced by the valet were the same size, colour, and shape, but were not his.

In the modern hotel shoes are cleaned either by a valet or a night porter.

The better hotels—indeed, only the best—put this duty on to the valets, who can collect the footwear for cleaning in their own service quarters. The majority of hotels, however—mainly those without a day valet service—use the night porter to attend to shoes. In a small hotel—up to fifty to seventy rooms—it is usual for shoes to be put in the corridor overnight for attention. At the Goring Hotel every room has a lobby, so that a valet can enter either by day or night to collect and clean shoes without disturbing the visitor.

Today, of course, quite different quick-drying and highly-glossed shoe polishes are used. Up to 1936 at this hotel we had a valet who insisted on cleaning shoes on the old 'mutton-bone' system, by which the toe-cap was 'boned' first with a really shiny mutton shin before finally being 'rubbed off'. These methods are now out of date. Some people lament their passing, but we must realize that today boots and shoes, although more flimsy in structure, are better cleaned and more quickly cleaned by modern methods. As mentioned elsewhere, wages have increased several hundred per cent. since 1918, so that it is essential to use quicker methods—always providing that these methods are efficient.

CHAPTER NINE

Weddings and Cakes

MY first wedding reception as Manager was the marriage of the daughter of Angela Barclay, who wrote a book called *The Rosary*, a best-seller in those days. My second was that of the niece of Admiral Lord Jellicoe.

Since then the Goring has become famous for its weddings. Our reception-rooms can be arranged to take small functions of ten people and, by a continuation of rooms, up to 250 people.

More thought and organization goes into the preparation of these receptions than the general public realizes. In the first place, it took quite a time to plan the best layouts in the early days: where to put the bride and groom, where to put the cake, and where to place the parents, etc.

For the information of brides and brides' mothers-to-be, let me make it clear that the hotel generally knows the best advantage to which reception-rooms can be adapted. It is good policy to separate the bride and bridegroom as far as possible from the parents receiving the guests. This may not be the usual procedure as some people understand it, but I have always found that it helps in the smooth running of the function.

To start with, if the bride and groom and parents all stand together at the door, the entrance to the reception-room becomes congested. Also, each guest wishes to speak in a different way to the parties concerned, according to their standing in the respective families. To separate the bride and groom from the door and to place them at a little further distance, with their wedding cake between them and possibly the bridesmaids beside them, therefore helps the smooth running of the function and it obviates a great deal of congestion. It is a trait of human nature to crowd together at a reception. Why, I cannot tell. This, of course, hinders the service of drinks and the passing of snacks, for the waiters cannot get through the throng, or, if they do, they are very liable to accidents. After such a function, guests go away with an indifferent opinion of the hotel's capabilities.

To spread out the guests is therefore a wise policy and this can only be achieved by a long approach to the reception-rooms when parents and the bridal couple can stand side by side), or by separating the bridal couple in order to 'draw' the expectant guests further into the room. For a similar reason, the buffet tables should be near a door, to allow service and replacement by waiters from behind the buffet rather than in front. To illustrate the importance of this point, I will draw from my own wide experience.

At the Goring we have two main reception-rooms. One holds from 100 up to 150 guests and the other about seventy-five guests. These rooms open into each other with double swing-doors. For a function of over 150 guests, therefore, both rooms are thrown open. Full buffets are placed in both rooms. The parents receive at the entrance to the smaller room and guests pass through to the bigger room to congratulate the bridal couple.

Within half an hour, however, the whole 175 to 200 guests have squeezed into the larger room and the smaller (and possibly more attractive) room is left empty, with the buffet almost untouched.

Our job is then to entice some of the guests from one room into the other, if only for the purpose of giving the staff breathing and moving space.

I look upon the smooth flow at wedding receptions as essential. I also consider my goodwill from these functions as very valuable. Many is the time I receive inquiries from wedding guests who have been to someone else's function at the Goring Hotel. Frankly, my best customers are mothers with three or more daughters. I have several families on my records who fulfil this happy condition, and I seem assured of weddings repeated by the same family on more than one occasion. We have now, of course, long ago reached the stage when daughters or sons are repeating the example of their parents in this matter of receptions.

One charming girl of a marriageable age called about her

wedding reception. She explained that her parents had been married at the Goring, and that her mother had told her she was conceived at the Goring, so what else could the poor girl do?

*

Not our best, but our most numerous, weddings took place during the war. At times we had as many as three weddings on the same day. On one occasion we managed a record of five.

These war weddings were difficult to handle. Apart from the scarcity of champagne, we also have to obtain permission to serve 'alcoholic drinks outside the permitted hours'. This implies an exemption of licence—issued by the police. And the police require a minimum notice of ten days to make the necessary inquiries. During those days, however, they made matters easier, and I often got my permit in three days—once in twenty-four hours.

It is surprising what one can do with wedding cakes. I always find out the background of the bridal couple. As a result, much pleasure and amusement can be afforded at a wedding. Apart from the ordinary coloured shields depicting naval, R.A.F., or regimental crests, great fun can be had in other directions.

I discovered once that the bridegroom worked at the Mint. His cake was smothered in golden sovereigns and silver shillings, made of chocolate and covered in gold and silver paper. Cakes, of course, can be made to any shape or size—round, square, oblong, diamond, triangular, oval, heart-shaped, etc. One gave me a great deal of trouble, for the bridegroom was an archaeologist. We settled for cuneiform tablets round the bottom layer, with a model excavation of the remains of a biblical city on the top layer.

Talking of cakes, I had the honour of supplying the official christening cake for our Prince Charles, Prince of Wales. A photograph of this cake appears amongst the illustrations. Its weight was about 75 lb., in two tiers. The sugar decoration was in four thicknesses of very fine, lace-like piping in a lattice pattern. This is extremely difficult to do, as each extra layer of piping must stand away from the one beneath it. The work took four days and was carried out by a master confectioner from Sheffield in a basement room at the Goring Hotel. Special flood-lights were fitted up for night work (it was late autumn) and two ladies' hair-driers were used to set the thin piping quickly, so that the thin layers of filigree work would not make contact or sag. Between the columns holding the bottom layer from the top layer were four small cribs, held in the beaks of storks. A silver representation of the Royal coat-of-arms incorporating several silver charms suitable for a young child adorned the top, while at the base was laid a copy of a Charles I feeding-spoon. This spoon was the workmanship of an old friend of mine who had taken up silvercraft as a hobby in his declining years. He was the proud owner of a private silver assay mark, and was one of only six people in England to have such a right in silvercraft outside the big goldsmith and silversmith firms.

At the time food restrictions were still in force, and great trouble was experienced in producing the necessary supply of raisins, sultanas, peels, etc., which were still under ration and only available in small quantities in the shops around Christmastime.

That year I happened to be Chairman of the Universal Cookery and Food Association, with Sir Piers Legh, Master of the King's Household, as President, and the Queen Mary the Queen Mother as Patron.

Having obtained permission to present the cake to Her Majesty Queen Elizabeth II (then H.R.H. Princess Elizabeth) through these exalted personages, I was still worried as to how to obtain the basic materials with which to make the cake. I therefore applied to all members of the Association personally to send any proper rich cake ingredients they could buy or spare. Over 100 lb. of ingredients were thus obtained, more than was actually required. This was all mixed and prepared, and the odd 30 lb. of cake mixture was made into several smaller cakes, iced, and presented to several children's hospitals named by Her Majesty Queen Elizabeth II.

CHAPTER TEN

Hotel Furnishings

NATURALLY, in the last fifty years bedroom furnishings have altered.

In 1910 the Goring Hotel opened with the old-type brass and iron bed in most bedrooms. These iron bedsteads had high tops and ends, with brass nobs—which came off—and were not very sightly by modern-day standards. Large, deep, cane-sided box springs built on wooden frames with a hair-and-wool overlay (mattress) went with them.

These mattresses, which some people call 'French style', were extremely comfortable and are still considered the best by many people. Unfortunately, they have a way of 'hardening up' after a couple of years. Being slept on by hundreds of different people, they never get the chance to settle to one person's shape. Remaking was a fairly costly job, and if accidents happened, these mattresses had to be often cleaned and remade before their turn for this treatment was normally due. I was never in favour of interior-sprung mattresses, for I have found that they wear unevenly and are very difficult to treat once the springs start getting weak.

For many years now the Goring Hotel has been equipped throughout with Dunlopillo mattresses, placed on the original countersunk cane-sided box springs. Dunlopillo are soft and pliable, can easily be cleaned, and are very long-wearing. One hospital in London has had them in constant use for twenty years, with no material upkeep.

The combination of cane-sided box springs with foam mattresses is ideal, and in my opinion better than the hard bases which are usually sold for use with Dunlopillo overlays today.

After the 1914-18 War, the first brass and iron bedsteads were replaced by square-tubed brass beds of a much more modern design, and these bedsteads are still in use. They have been relacquered once, and are still in excellent condition. Very solid, they do not need any upkeep and do not show wear and tear.

The brass bedstead really went out of vogue just before the war. In fact, for many years, from 1939 to about 1958, they were unobtainable and their manufacture seemed to have stopped. Today they are slowly coming back, but at a price which puts them out of competition with any other type of bed in popular demand.

From the beginning we have had a number of wooden beds of mahogany Sheridan design. These started off with heavy top frames—always coming unpegged. By a simple process, these top frames were removed some years ago, and now they look modern and up-to-date and have the advantage of looking very expensive.

All our beds are fitted with large size Vono angle castors, thus saving wear and tear on the carpets and making the beds easier to move about.

Wooden beds of various designs have always been popular, and will always remain so.

It is quite possible that many of my readers may have commented on the fact that very few hotel managers will have the second bed taken from a double room in single occupancy. The reason is simply explained by 'wear and tear'. To take a bed—especially a wooden bed—out of a bedroom will cause more wear and tear in two weeks through scratching and man-handling than by leaving the bed unused in a bedroom for one year.

Many people prefer a divan bed today, in view of the smaller room size of modern rooms. These, with a back-board, certainly save space, but are not very suitable for hotel use—although they are extensively used today. I find people use them too much as chairs and they are always untidy-looking and crumpled.

In 1910 a popular piece of furniture was the Beaconsfield—a combination piece of hanging cupboard, shelves, hat-shelf, and drawers. They are still extremely useful pieces of furniture, but times have moved on and rooms have become smaller, so that they now look too bulky.

Built-in furniture did not exist, with the possible exception of a few wardrobe cupboards. All furniture was solidly and expensively made to stand away from the wall. In those days furniture could be moved around—and it also had a second-hand value.

Today big furniture is a glut on the market as older houses are demolished and big bedrooms turned into smaller ones.

Central heating being almost unknown at the turn of the century, every room had to have a fireplace. The work of the floor staff in an hotel was very much more arduous. There were coals and wood to be taken to the various fireplaces, grates to clean and re-lay, slops had to be emptied, hot water had to be fetched in cans any time it was asked for, 'articles' under beds had to be attended to, and even hip-baths provided.

The taking of a hip-bath was an event. The carpet had to be covered with thick towels near the fireplace, the bath brought in and filled by hand to the right temperature and the fire lighted to give warmth. Afterwards the bath had to be emptied and removed and the bedroom put in order.

A chambermaid's wages in those days were 10s. per week, sleep in! Today, for much less work and shorter hours, the wages are eight times as much!

One of our problems was in connection with fireplaces. Bathrooms in those days had to have outside windows if they had w.cs. included (which they very seldom did), and the fireplace in a bedroom acted partly as ventilation. In fact, in many places local building by-laws insisted that hotel bedrooms should be built with opening fanlights over the doors if the bedroom had no chimney and fireplace.

As we all know, a fireplace takes up a lot of space, and its chimney breast upsets the contours in the wall of a room, so that furniture was difficult to fit in.

At the Goring Hotel we gradually overcame these 'old-fashioned' rooms by dispensing with the fireplaces and building wash-hand basins in the actual recess thus formed.

In some rooms we built in ladies' powder tables, thus making more floor space and doing away with odd, awkward-shaped pieces of furniture.

Recently we have scrapped whole rooms and built furniture right into the walls. This has had the effect of gaining more floor space, and has had a delightful effect on those untidy mantelpiece walls which worried us in the past. One now gets a pleasant vista of wardrobe, dressing table, writing table, and built-in drawers along one wall only. Also, the room is much easier to dust, and one saves a few yards of carpet per room where the furniture is built-in.

Carpets are another item of furnishing interest. In times gone by, large-pattern carpets in many colours and of scroll design were the fashion. These were often wasteful to lay, on account of matching the big pattern supplied in twenty-seven inch strips. These were followed by small-pattern carpets, often in a pine-shaped motif and with a ground of different colours. A range of such carpets was in vogue in 1914, and has just come back into fashion. I was surprised to see how many hotels use these same old patterns thinking they are designs of today.

Between the wars 'futurist', jazz, and cubist carpets became the rage. These seem to have been imported from France and Belgium.

Today very bright and small-patterned carpets are in vogue. At the Goring Hotel we had for many years a standard carpet with a small-motif, beige pine design on a blue ground. This was put into nearly every room in the hotel except the private sitting-rooms and public rooms. The reason for this choice was due to the fact that this particular carpet would not show ink-stains! Remember, people have not carried fountain pens and ball-point pens for so very many years. Our bedrooms still have drawers in the writing tables fitted for safety inkwells, and it used to be the housekeeper's job to change the nibs for each arriving guest. A great deal of expense was caused by guests in ways they do not even imagine. The spilling of ink on carpets and down wallpaper was amongst them.

Plain carpets are not popular in hotels; they tread-mark easily and show up every stain. Even when stains are rubbed out they leave a grey 'tide-mark', so that they always look uncared-for.

At the moment the Goring Hotel is going in for small-pattern, modern scroll motifs on rust and a two-tone, small-leaf design in red.

The days of the inkpot are gone, so we can break into a little more colour.

Wallpaper *versus* paint has always been a controversy. This we overcame by doing half the rooms in paint and half in wallpaper.

Square rooms look better in paint or panelled walls. Odd-shaped (chimney-breasted) rooms look better in paper.

Silver and china have altered over the years. Heavy, ornate table silver which was hard to keep clean has given way to smooth-surface table ware—very much more practical. A vogue for short-bladed knives for meat and game showed itself between the wars, but this has fortunately died out, for the design of the silverware was badly balanced and thus slightly uncomfortable to handle. Table silver should balance just over halfway down on spoons and forks, and near the joint of the blade and handle on a knife.

Thank heaven the three-pronged fork did not last long. A more difficult instrument to use is hard to imagine—except chopsticks!

We still have our old Kent's knife machine, which we occasionally use to get a polish on knife blades and to sharpen them.

The advent of stainless steel blades after the 1914-18 War was of great assistance. I can remember the old steel blades which took the rust and the egg-stains of the past. The knives had to go through the machine six at a time, or be rubbed on a knife board separately with Oakey's Wellington knife polish—a brown powder. This brown powder clung to everything on the knife handle and was difficult to get away from the shoulder of the knife. The disconcerting habit of guests at table polishing their knives and silver with their serviettes before eating (and generally getting a lot of dirt off them) was due largely to knife powder and the beaten-up soft soap which we used for cleaning silver.

The table silver today is much easier to keep clean with modern rinsing methods and burnishing machines than in the past. To illustrate the point, I used to employ three full-time silver-cleaners pre-war. Now, with three times the business, I employ two full-time men and my silver is very much cleaner.

Even the size of plates has changed. Previously we used a 12- to 14-inch meat plate with a large rim, or shoulder. Now we use a 10-inch standard plate, with a 7$\frac{1}{2}$-inch for side or cheese plate.

Some hotels use a shoulderless plate, but whether it is an advantage I would not like to argue. I imagine it would cause salt to fall into the wet gravy, and it tends to make the clearing away of plates more difficult for the waiter. However, it has the advantage of being 'something different'.

Walkie-talkie

The Goring Hotel claims to be the first hotel in the world to have installed a walkie-talkie system of staff control. For very many years—about forty-five—we had relied on a noisy front-door bell to announce arriving guests and call various staff if wanted. Thus an arriving guest was announced by one, or two rings to call a porter to take up the luggage, three rings to the maintenance, and four rings to the housekeepers to telephone for instructions.

This very loud bell—it had to be loud to reach most parts of the building—was situated in the lift shaft at middle-floor level, so that many of the guests had the 'benefit' of its clang by day and by night.

While all services have their telephone, and always have had, the employees concerned are not always available there, and may be doing duty in some other part of the house—having a meal, etc.

I had hated this noise for many years, and when I saw a report in a daily newspaper that a Mr. Foot had installed a walkie-talkie in a London hospital for just the same reason—noise—I at once approached him. The system really consists of a low-voltage relay wave, controlled by a live wire fixed on the outer wall all round the hotel. This relay carries about 15 yards in all directions, making a 30-yard span of a building.

It is suitable for square or oblong buildings, but buildings with courtyards (interior) would have to be doubly wired in order to get a good effect.

The relay system is controlled in the front hall by the hall porter, who, by an arrangement of buzzes, can speak to the staff concerned. The members of the staff concerned—about eight only—can thus be 'got at' in any part of the house. Each member of the staff carries a small battery receiving set, which is attached to his person, very much as a hearing aid. In fact, the whole system is worked on a hearing-aid principle, but enlarged.

As the guests can also hear what is said on the walkie-talkie, if conversing with a member of the staff, the control is in the front hall, so that the announcer must moderate his language when speaking. He is not so likely to use slang in front of visitors as he might do if his master set was in a back office.

It would have been much more convenient to have placed the 'master control' in the telephone exchange, but for the above reason. My decision was based on a conversation I once over-heard in a radio taxi: 'Go to 85 Park West. Old geyser says she only has a £5 note, so see you b—— well get it right.'

Staff talking to staff is not always the same as staff talking to visitors. . . .

This walkie-talkie has solved the noise problem. In fact, many guests comment on the 'third' conversation that seems to go on in their presence, but when the matter is explained their reaction is that it is a good idea.

The drawback is that it is only a one-way device, so that a code had to be devised on the same lines as the old clanging bell. Each person concerned must remember his 'bell code' and need only listen when his number of pips 'pip'.

Things like (two pips) 'Valets go to front hall arrival', (four pips) 'Housekeeper arrange special flowers, arrival, Room 114', (three pips) 'Maintenance, attention light switch, No. 86', all save time and unnecessary walking about. Previously staff had to be found, brought to our office to receive instructions, and then return to their place of duty.

There is a humorous side to almost everything in an hotel if one looks for it, and walkie-talkie is no exception. We got the humorous side within a few weeks of starting our new idea. A small luncheon party was taking place in a private room amongst some very important steel directors, one of whom was deaf.

Halfway through the meal he turned irritably to his neighbour and said: 'This is a conference on steel, so why keep talking about luggage up, and giving pips? What's it all about?'

Thus we found out that our new installation was only a glorified hearing aid, on the same low wavelength, and got the firm to alter it.

Another amusing incident was in connection with the Fire Brigade. One day a small fire broke out in a building opposite the hotel, and the Fire Brigade was sent for. The firemen entered the building and left their fire float empty.

Within minutes we heard from across the road: (four pips) 'Housekeeper, flowers in No. 67, please.'

This, of course, made us all roar with laughter, for we had not realized that our installation was the same low wavelength as that used by the Fire Brigade, and we have not bothered to tell them, hoping that another fire will not take place in such close proximity.

While many hospitals now have this system installed, I understand that it is not used as we use ours, for it puts doctors off their work to have to listen to all sorts of conversations while attending patients, and they prefer to use it at meal hours only, when they are away from the wards.

CHAPTER ELEVEN

The Visitors' Book

It is a matter of regret to me that the Goring Hotel never had a Visitors' Book in the earlier days. I suppose my father never realized the interest and importance such a book could command. For instance, the autographs of the Royal Household visitors to the Coronation of King George V could have been preserved, and the other occasions—such as the visit of Kaiser Wilhelm II of Germany with his staff in 1912—would have made our Visitors' Book almost priceless in memories of byegone days.

My father never expected his Goring Hotel to be so successful as it ultimately has become, so that these memories are lost to us.

Under protest from my father, I bought a fine leather-covered and tooled Visitors' Book in 1934 in time for the occasion of the marriage of the Duke of Kent to Princess Marina of Greece, and I am still very pleased with this purchase.

Only about twenty pages of our Visitors' Book have so far been used since 1934, but the quality of the entire entries must be almost unique. Only our very influential guests are asked to sign, and the book is only used a few times in each year.

We start in 1934 at the Duke of Kent's wedding with the signatures of Lord and Lady Craigavon, old friends of our family, who actually lived two doors away from us in Victoria Square. After a distinguished career in Northern Ireland as Major Craig (later Sir James Craig), Lord Craigavon was the first Lord Lieutenant of Northern Ireland.

On the occasion of the same wedding we had staying with us the Dame of Honour to Princess Nicolas of Greece, Madame Tombazi, with her husband, who was a high Court official. Also

Mr. Grouitch and Baron Antitch, Marshal of the Court and Minister of the Court to the King of Yugoslavia respectively. Count Trampe, Chamberlain to the King of Denmark, was also a guest on this occasion, as was Countess Pontappidan, the Lady-in-Waiting to the Queen of Denmark. There is also a lone signature—C. A. Cambrensis, Archbishop of Wales (Dr. Green), who had promised to officiate at my own wedding the previous year. Unfortunately, his wife was very ill at the time and died very shortly afterwards.

The next two pages of our book are devoted to a variety of celebrities who visited the hotel between 1934 and 1936. Amongst these well-known persons are Lord Clyde, Admiral of the Fleet Sir Roger and Lady Keyes, Lord Pollington, John Drinkwater, Lord and Lady Mottistone, General Sir H. and Lady Hudson, Sir Adrian Boult, Prince and Princess Viggo, Countess Blucher of Wahlstadt, Lord Ashcombe, Lord and Lady Fisher, the Earl of Albemarle, Lord Holmpatrick, William Tilden, Jnr. (Tennis Champion at Wimbledon), Lady Olga Montagu, Prince Peter of Greece, the Countess of Clonmell, Field-Marshal Lord Birdwood, Sir Austen and Lady Chamberlain, Sir William Gentle, the Earl of Shrewsbury, Lady Mary Hartington, Air Commodore Sutton, Sir Frederick Heygate, Sir Philip Game, Rear-Admiral Scott Land, U.S.N., Lady Hardinge, Sir Hughe Knatchbull-Hugessen, Sir Arthur Longmore, Lord Willingdon, Lord Chelmsford, and Prince Hohenzollern.

Most of these guests were known to me personally. For instance, Sir Roger Keyes was a regular guest, who reminded me of the fact that I was in Dover at the time of the famous Zeebrugge Raid during the First World War and saw the warships leave and come back to Dover at that time.

John Drinkwater, a famous man of letters and so respected on the Isle of Man, was a visitor with whom I often had a conversation.

Lord and Lady Mottistone were very old visitors and friends—right back to the time of the formation of our first Royal Flying Corps. Lord Mottistone—possibly better known as General Seely—was our first ever Minister of Aviation before the First World War.

He delighted in telling the story of his arrival at the Goring Hotel on one occasion during that period: 'I got in from France in a disgusting state. One of your valets put me, fully clothed, into a hot bath to 'soften me up' and then proceeded to delouse me.'

Sir Adrian Boult has been a friend since 1935. For many years he had a large apartment at Whitehall Court, but recently—owing to ill health and respiratory trouble—he has had to leave his apartment on the Thames-side and find other accommodation at a higher level away from the Thames fog and damp. He did me the honour to consult me first in the choosing of his new home, but unfortunately I was unable to help him—for he has a positive library of music, filling many bookcases, of the scores to which he must, naturally, refer. In 1948 he was kind enough to consent to conduct his Philharmonic Orchestra at the Albert Hall in honour of the visiting members of the International Hotel Association, who were attending a congress in London.

Prince and Princess Viggo of Denmark spent their honeymoon at the Goring Hotel many years ago. Princess Viggo used to come to London once or twice a year in order to spend a day or so with H.M. Queen Mary at Marlborough House. Her Highness still comes to London each year, and generally manages to spend a night at our country house at Wrotham.

In return, I have visited Prince Viggo in his very fine residence outside Copenhagen.

Prince Peter of Greece has always intrigued me by his friendly approach. We were corresponding at one time during the period between the wars, and to clinch our correspondence regarding accommodation he sent a typical telegram: 'O.K. Prince Peter.'

As a young man, Nelson Eddy used to come from America each year with his mother. He was only just starting in the film world and was quite unknown. When he became world-famous and, incidentally, very rich, he frequented the more expensive hotels in London. I was rather pleased, because he had a noisy habit of lying in a hot bath and letting it overflow for an hour at a time while practising scales at the top of his voice. He was very amazed when one day I had to send someone up to his apartment to get him out of the bath in order to answer the telephone, so that I could tell him not to make so much noise. His bathing habits were irregular—sometimes at midday and sometimes at midnight.

Sir Austen and Lady Chamberlain, as I have mentioned elsewhere in this book, lived at the Goring Hotel for over two years, and the hotel thus became a veritable Parliamentary and diplomatic centre. Mr. (later Sir) Anthony Eden, then Foreign Secretary, used to call almost daily to discuss the sanctions problems raised by the Italian-Abyssinian War. Sir Austen Chamberlain never got on with his half-brother Neville Chamberlain. Each morning Neville would walk down Lower Grosvenor Place—within sight of his brother's bedroom window—on his way to the House of Commons. I do not once remember his entering the Goring for a friendly chat.

Sir Hughe Knatchbull-Hugessen, who was our Ambassador to China in 1936-7, was a regular visitor. Many of us remember that he was 'shot up' in his official car in China and, being wounded, was given leave, which he spent partly at the Goring Hotel. Later he became Ambassador to Turkey during the Second World War.

Sir Arthur Longmore, one of our first Air leaders in the First World War, still visits us in his capacity as Chief of the War Graves Commission.

Lord and Lady Willingdon were regular guests. This was before and after Lord Willingdon became the Viceroy of India. Their son, Viscount Rattendon, occupied No. 9 Victoria Square for some years, and after their retirement the Willingdons were again constant visitors. Lord Willingdon died many years ago, but Lady Willingdon came to the hotel for meals up to the time of her death in 1959.

Lady Mary Hartington of the Devonshire family admitted to me that she felt somewhat nervous, as it was the first time in her life that she had slept in an hotel. I have every reason to believe she slept soundly and took away a good impression of hotels in general.

Then came the Coronation of King George VI in 1937. Our Visitors' Book shows the long list of visitors for whom accommodation was reserved by Buckingham Palace. The list is headed by the Crown Prince of Norway (at that time) and Princess Marthe. They confided to me that they were so pleased to be at the Goring Hotel, as they at least got a private bathroom, which Buckingham Palace was quite incapable of providing! Naturally, their Lady-in-Waiting and Aide-de-Camp occupied rooms close by.

We also had the Marshal of the Court and the Lady-in-Waiting to the Swedish Crown Prince. Also the Lady-in-Waiting and the Grand Master to the Household of Princess Juliana of the Netherlands.

I asked Baron Rengers, the Grand Master, why, when he attended functions in his Court uniform, he had a large silver key attached to his person in a very prominent position at his left hip. He told me that it was the 'key to the cashbox'—'but it does not fit our present strongroom'—he replied.

We also had staying with us Lieut.-General Christitch, A.D.C. to the King of Yugoslavia, and Countess Loganitch, Lady of Honour to Princess Paul of Yugoslavia. The Yugoslavian Royal Family were accompanied by a special detective. He was a very swarthy-looking man with black hair and very, very heavy moustachios—the real fierce, gangster, nineteenth-century brigand type. He did not appear to have much to do, and enjoyed his 'holiday on official business' by taking a bottle of brandy and a 7-lb. tin of biscuits to bed with him each night. With that, and his bottle of wine with every meal, he did himself well, but I wonder if he would have been capable enough to attend to any detective business had he been called upon to do so. Actually, I suppose his eating habits did not matter very much, as the bill was paid by Buckingham Palace (the King's Privy Purse) in any event.

The Greek delegation at the Goring Hotel was represented by that fabulous figure, Count Mercati, with the Captain-General to the Crown Prince of Greece.

Amongst others staying in the hotel at the time was Dr. Julius Lippert, Oberburgermeister of Berlin.

*

In the two short years between the Coronation of King George VI and the outbreak of war, I note the following names in my Visitors' Book:

Lady Mary Montagu (sister of Lady Olga Montagu), the Marquis of Abergavenny, Admiral Sir Reginald Tyrwhitt, Lord Hawke, Lord Hugh Cecil, Pierre Cot, Philip Noel Baker, and Dr. Beneš, that ill-fated Czechoslovak Prime Minister. At that time we also had Herr Henlein, Hitler's puppet before the overrunning of Czechoslovakia (we did not advertise this fact for political reasons).

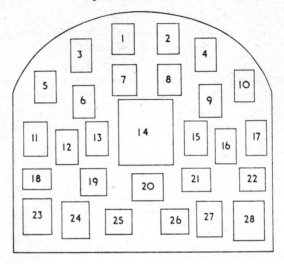

1. Mrs. Charrington.

2. Brigadier H. V. S. Charrington, D.S.O., M.C.

3. Miss Neergaard, Lady-in-Waiting to H.R.H. Princess Margaretha of Denmark.
Captain Wern, Master of Ceremonies to H.R.H. Prince Axel of Denmark.
Captain Neville, R.N.

4. Madam Ostgaard, Lady-in-Waiting to H.R.H. the Crown Princess of Norway.
Commander Stang, Aide-de-Camp to H.R.H. the Crown Prince of Norway.

5. Lady Leigh.
Lady Ashton of Hyde.

6. Count Mercati, Lord Chamberlain to the Court of Greece.

7. Monsieur D. N. Levidis, Grand Marshal of the Court of Greece.

8. H.R.H. Princess Marie of Greece.
H.R.H. Prince George of Greece.

9. Admiral of the Fleet, Viscount Cunningham of Hyndhope, K.T., G.C.B., O.M.
Viscountess Cunningham.

10. His Honour Judge Essenhigh.
Mrs. Essenhigh.

11. Lady Fisher.
Lord Fisher of Kilverstone.

12. Mrs. Longden, Her Worship the Mayor of Sheffield.
Miss Longden.

13. His Grace the Archbishop of Wales.

14. Mr. O. R. Goring—1869–1948. Founded this Hotel in 1910. The first Hotel in the world with private bathroom and central heating to every bedroom.

15. H.S.H. Princess Agnes of Leichtenstein.
H.S.H. Prince Charles of Liechtenstein.

16. Mrs. Hume.
His Worship the Mayor of Vancouver, B.C.

17. Lady Dunleath.
The Rt. Hon. Lord Dunleath, C.B.E. D.S.O.

18. Baroness Van Heemster, Lady-in-Waiting to H.R.H. Princess Juliana of the Netherlands.
Baron Van Burmania Rengers, Grand Master of the Household of H.R.H. Princess Juliana of the Netherlands.

19. Heer Ostgaard, Aide-de-Camp to H.R.H. the Crown Prince of Norway.

Count Rudebeck, Marshal of the Court to H.R.H. the Crown Prince of Sweden.

Adm. Sir Henry Buller, G.C.V.O., C.B.

Madam Ostgaard, Lady-in-Waiting to H.R.H. the Crown Princess of Norway.

Countess Reutersward, Lady-in-Wait-in to H.R.H. the Crown Princess of Sweden.

20. H.R.H. the Duke of Edinburgh.

Mr. O. G. Goring. (November, 1957)

21. H.R.H. Princess Marie of Greece.

Admiral Selby.

H.R.H. Prince George of Greece.

Monsieur D. N. Levidis.

22. The Hon. Robert Corbett.

Lady Rowallan.

The Rt. Hon. Lord Rowallan, K.B.E., M.C., the Chief Scout.

The Hon. Fiona Corbett.

23. Viscountess Craigavon.

The Rt. Hon. Viscount Craigavon, First Premier of Northern Ireland.

24. The Goring Hotel Souvenir Pro-gramme of the Coronation of their Majesties King George VI and Queen Elizabeth, 12th May, 1937.

25. Countess Reuterswald, Lady-in-Wait-ing to H.R.H. the Crown Princess of Sweden.

Count Rudebeck, Marshal of the Court to H.R.H. the Crown Prince of Sweden.

Adm. Sir Henry Buller, G.C.V.O., C.B.

26. Colonel Severac, Aide-de-Camp.

Count D'Aillieres.

H.S.H. Prince Pierre of Monaco.

General Sir Sidney Clive.

27. The Goring Hotel Souvenir Pro-gramme of the Coronation of Her Majesty Queen Elizabeth II.

28. Official christening cake made for H.R.H. the Prince of Wales, at the Goring Hotel—Nov., 1948.

Wilmington

Sept. 1536

Marie Dilling Ahr

Walton Castle
Kent.

Jan. 6th — 1887.

Chelmsford

[signature]

Maud
Crown Princess of Norway.

May 4th — 8th 1937

Olav Crown Prince of Norway

Ragni Østgaard Lady in waiting
to H. R. H. The Crown Princess of Norway

Østgaard . Aide - de - Camp
to H. R. H. The Crown Prince of Norway.

Smörgåsbord /
Lady in waiting to H.R.H. the Crown Princess of Sweden

(Mlle Ida Delbeeck.)
Marshal of the Court to H.R.H. the Crown Prince of Sweden.

Henry Nelles.
attached to T.R.H. The Crown Prince + Crown Princess of Sweden.

Mr E.J. Van Holthe. Lieut. Comdr Royal Netherland Navy, A.D.C. to
H.M. the Queen of Holland.

Sq. Ldr C. Baumann.   Royal Guest his Excell.   A.D.C. to H.R.H. the Crown Prince of Spain.

Captain N.R. Høysted - Air Attaché - ADC to H.R.H the
Antith. Minister of the Court   Crown Prince of Sweden.

Agatha Luckhof

Baroness M.J. Van Steenstra
Lady in waiting to H.R.H. The Princess Juliana
of the Netherlands.

Baron von Boetzelaer Rengers.
Grand Master to the Household of H.R.H. Princess Juliana of the
C. E. Longuère. Lord Mayor of Sheffield 1937   Netherlands.

G. Schiaroncki, captain R.H.A. A.D.C. to H.R.H. the Crown Prince of Sweden.

Lord Gerald W. Churchill. C.V.O. M.C. Swiss Ministre-gerant to H.M. the King of Yugoslavia's

Grigorith. Dame d'honneur de H.A.R.H. la Princesse Paul de Yugoslavie

Accessiti

Doris Marla Park

Kharakhalisorboth   Hassel Nadoliczange 8
Oena Nikolaie — Pombriano Kr
and my niece

Dr. Julius Tippert. Oberst 2 Moult & Berlin.
Liume Schulamn.

Dr. Mr. Kerr   Engineering Dr. Saw.   Sweden.

Lady Mary Herbert
Marquess & Marchioness of Abergavenny
Reginald Gwel? ?? #F
Kansas.
Cecil
h̄ Col
Philip's Mont Dorem

Stretton Hall Ashborne Derbyshire —
?? Stones. Larnat
Studli H. Kew K Lane.
Lippington Perry Coombe.
16 Southerton Place !
13 rue d'Orléans . Paris -
73 S. Gom Mar, Lisbon 141.

Shaun Bernep

Reginald Wingate gunal

1941 — Catherine Leslie Wingate —
AJWhitworth
HoryWR Koyp
R.K. L. Le??g
??Gray

Czechoslovakia
Prague.
Vinclenlair — Dunbar
SCOTLAND
"
"
Barlino . Slaughter . Sussex.
Rupigvork — Iceland.

Craigavon

Cecil Craigavon

E. R. Toudale Major d'hommage to S.M. le Roi, Maréchal de Knesa Nicolai de Grèce

Jacques Fouchas

Hasso v. Gravenitz Maréchal de la Cour de S.M. le Roi de Yougoslavie

John Astitt, Ministre de la Cour de S.M. le Roi de Yougoslavie 1902

... Vicomond Royal Danish Navy

G. Steger Colonel et Chambellan Chef de la Maison militaire de S.A. le Roi le Danemark

Count Joringo Chamberlain Master of Ceremonies to H.M. the King of Denmark

Vivin Soriee

Anna Pavlopsidarí lady in waiting to the Queen of
Roumania.

Malagola

Edohel Esmuella to the Danish legation.

Admiral of the Fleet Sir Roger and Lady Keyes

Ethel Ivanikaña

Mottistone

Evelyn Mottistone

Guestbook —

General Sir Hereward Wake, Baronet.

General's wife, Margaret Wake.

Stanley Baldwin —

Frances Vigo.

Eleanor Brennan 1930.

Countess Blanche of Wahldall

Adrian —
Countess of Portumaale
Earl of Altbrook
wife active —

Wm. J. Jordan 2nd.

Olga Walzin.

S. — Grace
A. Channell.
Countess of Channell.
Sir Arthur Henry Cochrane.
Countess Muriel Scherr–Thors
Sidworth.
Lancelto Birchwood.

Leonard Dunning
Joy Chamberlain
Austin Chamberlain.
William Joyce.
Emma R. Wilson ———
Ann R. Wy.

Earl of Shaftesbury

Adml. Sir R. Bray...

Harcourt...

Prince de Marienich

Lt. Col. T. Walton

Fred G. Hugatt...

J. S. French

Philip Sassoon

Envoy first and (?) Envoy
Red-admiral (C.C.)

Maj. Gen. Hardinge

Violet Hawtrey

Ivo Rosario

M. Clyde

1759 (?) Argyle Kentish? Bergam 1900

Arthur de Langmore....

Coronation of Her Majesty

George
Prince of Greece
Pres.t of Denmark

Marie
Princess George of Greece
née Bonaparte

Nicholas Larisch

Grand Marshal of the Grand R. Court
Athens.

Ragni Østgaard
Lady in-waiting to
H.R.H. The Crown Princess of Norway

Andr. Stang
Commander R.N.
Equerry & A.D.C. to H.R.H. The Crown Prince of Norway.

Windsor
Equerry to H.R.H. Prince George of Greece
A.D.C. to

Kjell W.R.
Commander R.D.N.
Naval of Permission to H.R.N. the King of Denmark

Christian
Won in 1 to
The Queen of Denmark.

Queen Elizabeth II.   2nd June 1953.

Elizabeth R

Princess dupus of discussion.

Prince Charles Alfred of distinction.

Prince of Hyde...

Rt. Hans Cuardl, Munich
27.3.58.

R.M Amadu

Margarita Princess of Hohenlohe Langenburg
Princess of Greece

Sophie
Princess George of Hanover
Princess of Greece

B.S./Alwadthia.   Lieutenant Sirena ? Tisey.

Hugh Macmillan —

David Finlay

Maro Rice

Martin Clark

W. Drummond

Rian

Duncan Sandys —

Allen

Smith W. Blackburn

Ashley Clarke

Geoffrey Hutto.

Price.

Garuk Rice

Chapman Andrew Taylor

Charles Little   Thakeham Street. Sussex.

28/7/42

Arthur ? Harris AM

signature

July 1943 ~ John C. Winant   Ambassador U.S.A

"   "   ~ Rt. Hon. Herbert Stanley Morrison, J.P. M.P ~ Secretary of State

for Home Affairs

"   "   ~ Philip Noel Baker, M.P.

"   "   ~ Lt. William George Sheldon Dobbie. C.B. C.M.G. D.S.O. ~ Governor

General of Malta.

signature S. Kosanik

major general

C.G.S. polish army

H. A. Helmut

Dec. 1945

Prime Minister.

25/1/1946

Norwegian Foreign Minister
SECRETARY of UNO

Zealand War

Julian Huxley
British School, Unesco
20-4/3/47.

Winchester

M.A. Choë

Assistant Secretary of Symallop

Prince of Luxembourg

John Green.

& Eric Fullerton

Vivian Eastwood

John Macpherson

Fr. Hans Moranz 22-24. III. 54
Munich

R.M.A. Hankey 28-VI-54 to 1-VII-54

Beatriz del Bustos Pubeniz
Infanta de España 14-10-52

Maria Elvira 22/10/52
2 March 53.

Mayor 29 Avenue Vancouver BC
Canada

William Kempf

Mayor Stevens 26/1 - 17/11/54

29/-11/1954.

+ B Carol Griffin

1958

Convocation of Lambeth.

Wm. P. Barrett — Suffr. Bishop —
F. H. Mehalason

Frederick Warnecke   Bishop of Rivers To
Frederick D. Goodwin   Bishop of Bethlehem
J. Rankin Wyatt   Bishop of Virginia
Gordon Reese   Bishop of Wyoming
Thomas H. Wright   Bishop of ...
Dudley Scott Stark   Bishop of ... (Rochester)
Malcolm E. Peabody   Bishop of Rochester, U.S.A.
    Bishop of Connecticut
Elwood L. Haines   Bishop of S.W. Florida
Geo. P. Gunn   Bishop of Texas

Henry K. Sherrill   Vice President of the National Council of the Protestant Episcopal Church
Roland J. Frank   Bishop of Saskatchewan
Leland Stark   Bishop Coadjutor of Newark
W. Higham   Bishop of Michigan
Randolph R. Claiborne Jr   Bishop of Southern Ohio   Cincinnati Ohio
    Bishop of Atlanta
Albert R. Stuart   Bishop of Georgia   Savannah, Ga. USA.
H. R. McAdoo   Bishop of Ohio   Cleveland Ohio USA
George P. Snell   Suffragan Bishop of Toronto

Margaretha Hofsteen
Lady in Waiting to H.H. the
Queen of the Netherlands.
Nov. 1947

Dmitri N. Levisi
Grand Maître des Cérémonies to H.M. the King of the
Netherlands.
The Hague. Holland.

Paul Lebeufy Maréchal de la cour de S.M. La Reine. By Hollins

G.A.D. Baron van Hardenbroek Grand Master of Ceremonies to H.M. the Queen of the Netherlands.

Waterapp van's Gravendeel.

Cairlinus — ADC to H.R.H. Prince Bernhard of the Netherlands.

Maurice Sicard

During the war our guests included the Grand Duchess Xenia of Russia, General Schuiter, U.S., Rear-Admiral Martin, Sir Odo Russell, our Ambassador to The Hague, Berne, and elsewhere, Sir Edward Marsh, Vice-Admiral Denis Boyd, Lord Clive, and others. Air Vice-Marshal R. Graham was a regular visitor, as was his boss, Air Marshal 'Bomber' Harris.

Peace having been re-established, our clientele changed again. One of our most regular visitors now became Trygve Lie, Norwegian Foreign Minister and General Secretary of U.N.O.

Julian Huxley also signed our book, as did the Duke of Norfolk, the Marquis of Winchester, Prince Felix of Luxembourg, and Eugene, Princess of Greece.

Now 1947 saw another official reception at Buckingham Palace, this time for the visit of the Greek Royal Family. Guests at the Goring Hotel included the Lady-in-Waiting to the Queen of the Hellenes, Count Levidi, Grand Master of Ceremonies to the Greek Court, and also Count Lelonday, Marshal to the Court. On this occasion we also had the Grand Master of Ceremonies to the Queen of the Netherlands, and also the A.D.C. to Prince Bernhard.

*

At the first Convocation of Lambeth after the war—in 1948—we became the headquarters of eleven American bishops. Their names appear on the plate from the Visitors' Book.

*

Between 1948 and the Coronation of Queen Elizabeth II, I find the following names in my Visitors' Book:

The Hon. M. H. Oram, Speaker of the House of Representatives, New Zealand; Harold E. Sexton, Bishop of British Columbia; H. J. Bird, Justice of Appeal, British Columbia; Lord de Lisle and Dudley, V.C., Secretary of State for Air, 1951-5; Major-General Sir Hubert Rance, Governor of Trinidad and Tobago, 1950-5; Field-Marshal Sir William Slim, former Governor-General of Australia; General Sir Miles Dempsey; Lieut.-General Sir Leslie Morshead, President of the Bank of New South Wales; the Rt. Hon. Sir Ulick Alexander, Equerry to the Queen; Lieut.-General Sir Ralph Eastwood, Governor of Gibraltar, 1944-7; Princess Beatriz de Bourbon Torlonia, Infanta of Spain, who used to visit the hotel often whilst her daughter was at school in England; the Marquess of Conyngham; the Mayor of Vancouver (Mr. J. F. Hume); and last, but by no means least, on the page is His Eminence the late Cardinal Griffin, Archbishop of Westminster. Field-Marshal Sir William Slim apparently received his appointment to Australia somewhat suddenly—for Lady Slim asked me to aid in disposing of her new house near Oxted, Surrey, which she was just in the process of furnishing.

Turning to the Coronation of H.M. Queen Elizabeth II on 2nd June, 1953, our Visitors' Book shows a galaxy of names. We begin with George, Prince of Greece and Denmark, and his Consort, Princess Clare of Greece (*née* Bonaparte). Count Levidis was Grand Marshal of the Greek Court, and Rear-Admiral Vandoros was A.D.C. to Prince George on that occasion.

The Royal Family of Denmark was represented by the Master of Ceremonies and the Lady-in-Waiting to the Queen of Denmark.

Prince Charles of Liechenstein and Princess Alice were also our guests, as was H.S.H. Prince Pierre of Monaco, father of Prince Rainier. Prince Axel of Denmark visited us for the second time, for he had also attended the Coronation of King George VI.

Coming back to Prince Viggo of Denmark, I remember that when I was staying at his residence outside Copenhagen, he was driving me to his home when his car nearly hit another car. 'Oh, that's my brother, Axel,' he said. 'Always drives recklessly.'

Prince Axel is a great Rotarian. I have been to Rotary Clubs in Denmark which he has attended, and in fact he was President of the Rotary Club of Strandbaard, outside Copenhagen.

*

I also have in my Visitors' Book the signatures of Margarita, Princess of Hohenlohe Langenberg (Princess of Greece), and Sophia, Princess George of Hanover (Princess of Greece).

My readers will see that our connection with the Greek Royal Family is very marked. Actually, Prince Philip visited the Goring Hotel not so long ago, and I had the pleasure and honour of being presented to him.

Other signatures include those of Lord Attlee, Labour Prime Minister, Mr. Harold Macmillan, our present Prime Minister— these two of opposite parties have signed side by side—Lord Mills, Sir Kenneth Blackburn, Governor of Jamaica, Sir David Eccles, and Mr. Duncan Sandys.

CHAPTER TWELVE

Mainly Personal

In the autumn of 1919, I was already in Paris with the object of forgetting my schoolboy French, prior to taking a *cours* at the Ecole Hotelière, Lausanne.

I joined the Swiss Hotel School at Lausanne in January 1920 as an extern in the kitchen class. In those days, the new wing and the new dormitory house had not been built, so that about thirty of a total of ninety students slept out. The curriculum was much the same as at any of our hotel schools in England today, and consisted of preparing and cooking meals for ninety students, plus masters, plus staff. A nice little hotel of just over 100 people.

Afternoons were spent in menu construction, costing, and quantity control, including kitchen account books, dry stores control, tradesmen's accounts (the real ones—not theory) and other bookwork on the 'control' side. The class consisted of only ten pupils, which was lucky, as I got more individual attention from a well-qualified chef-teacher. The brigade was divided into five *parties—saucier, entremetier, rotisseur, garde manger, and patissier*. We were two to each *partie*, and changed over once a week on a rota system.

Market Day

Saturday mornings were 'market day'—our great adventure. The class would accompany the chef to buy the vegetables, fruit, and comestibles for the following week (we had cold storage installed) in the famous Lausanne Market, which occupies street

132

upon narrow street filled with peasant stalls in the old part of the
town, and even spreads out over the great Place de L'Université.
Vegetables and eggs were in one section, meat in another, while
University Square was the cheese market—of national repute.
The market is closed at 10 a.m. by police regulation, to allow
traffic to circulate through the narrow streets.

Now, all this sounds very simple and pleasant, until I tell you
that the *cour* was being held on the level of Lac Leman, and the
Lausanne Market is about 400 feet above it and reached only by
steep and winding roads. Furthermore, we had to take our *char*.
A *char* is a special wooden vehicle on four large wheels, with a
fairly large platform, and a long shaft in front, with a cross bar—
obviously intended to be used by two men. It is peculiar to
Switzerland in that form, but has near counterparts in Holland
and Belgium, where dogs assist in pulling. Holland and Belgium
are flat, however, whilst Switzerland is not. Besides, we had no
dog-power, but we did have the usual kitchen porter (international type), who invariably gave up as we reached the first
bend on the first hill!

Out at 7 a.m. with the prospect of pushing the *char* up the hills
might put some people off the job, but not keen youngsters in
their early twenties. Our reward came when, all our purchases
made, we could mount the *char* and toboggan home (wisely, we
invented a system of braking), leaving the chef and his kitchen
porter to descend on foot.

Arriving back at our kitchen, we were soon frenziedly un-
loading and changing into our white clothes, ready for the lunch
preparation.

Commis Waiter

It is not my intention to talk further on Lausanne, as the object
behind these reminiscences is to show what fun a care-free
student-employee can have if he is a good mixer. I only took the
kitchen course, as I considered the bookkeeper-receptionist and
waiting course superfluous.

So in June I got a job as *commis* waiter at the Villars Palace,
Villars-sur-Ollon, way up in the mountains in the Canton de
Valais. The fact that I had no experience did not seem to worry

the management. It was my English they were after, I suspect. Wages, 30 Swiss francs (25s.) per month, all found, and share in the *tronc*.

After an anxious journey, I reached Villars (two hours in a funicular from the main line) in time for supper at 6 p.m. What a nervous experience to enter a long pantry with a long table filled with about forty staff of all grades—a new boy, not too good at the language and with no practical background!

The Villars Palace was just opening for the summer season. This is a process unknown in England. It consists of getting the 'core' of the winter season staff (if they will come) to return early, to unparcel the beds, bedding, furniture, china, etc., which are methodically wrapped up at the end of every season. This, and general cleaning, takes several weeks, but rooms are prepared by floors working upwards, so that some accommodation is available for early season visitors.

The early incoming waiting staff are therefore not waiters at all. Their first job is to clean the very large plate-glass restaurant and *salle à manger* windows, and to re-surface the parquet floors.

In these days of electric parquet-cleaners, I presume this is easy, but in those days it meant steel-wool shavings, worked by the feet, up and down the room, in line with the herring-bone pattern of the flooring. About eight of us *commis and chefs de rang* were on this job for so many hours a day for two or three days. Our relaxation was hay-making on the hotel farm. Great fun, at which maids and men alike joined in.

Just before we 'got busy', the whole staff, about sixty by now, took a midnight trip up to the Chammosaire, another funicular run of three-quarters of an hour to a mountain-top. The snag was that the funicular had not yet started its seasonal operations. But why worry about that? Sixty people climbing a funicular track at midnight, arm in arm and singing as only the Swiss know how, is after all very stimulating. Especially as the café-owner at the top had 'opened up' with hot coffee, schnapps, and cakes. He could not have helped hearing us come.

Sunrise at 4 a.m. on the mountain-top, amongst the edelweiss, some way above the café was most inspiring. I was 'off' the next day, so, instead of returning with the rest, three of us found three of the girls who were also off duty, and spent the day tramping miles along the mountain-paths and goat-tracks. We returned about 5 p.m. with sore feet and quite exhausted; but I, at least, was pleased with the experience.

Staff Food

An hotel of over 200 rooms, with sixty staff and no guests, cannot be making much money. The management is therefore hard put to keep expenses down. Staff food suffers as a natural consequence. Ours was 'lousy'. Macaroni cheese, sphaghetti, rye bread, and eggs from the farm had been the staple diet during the first few weeks. The entire lack of meat (boiled beef once a week only) was expected by these seasonal workers, who quite understood management difficulties, and were themselves only waiting to earn tips. But when the season 'got going' in July and the feeding conditions did not improve, the fat was in the fire.

One night we were served with our *macaroni au gratin*, followed by what appeared to be perfect *doyen de comice* pears. Alas, they were all rotten in the middle. There had been a good deal of growling for the last few days, and now it suddenly reached a climax by someone throwing an overripe pear at the white-washed staff-room wall. This slushy brown imprint on the white wall was an immediate sign. Within two minutes thirty to forty pears were thrown in the same direction.

The pears were on the wall; there was no escape. The three ring-leaders, including an under-head waiter who had worked at the Berkeley, London, as a 'black-tie', were sent for by the management. They proved truculent, and unfortunately were addressing 'a management' who was known for his too stern control. The best terms they could get was to clean off and distemper the staff hall walls and pay the bill. They refused. The next day they started a strike committee and openly stated their intention of walking out on 1st August. The management held on, thinking that it was too late in the season for them to find other employment.

On 1st August, the most notable Swiss holiday of the year, and with a packed house of over 300 guests expecting a *Soirée de Gala*, they walked out.

Our stern and ruthless 'management' almost cried at the sight of his waiting staff and most of his cooks leaving him. We were all lined up, and as each passed by he or she was asked if he intended to stay. Having a British passport and still being somewhat raw, I do not think I was expected to strike, and was not approached. In any case, I stayed on. That midnight I was left alone to clear a large restaurant single-handed, having tried to serve meals all day, with only two *chefs de rang* left. Very tired, I piled my last tray with valuable dessert plates, china fruit bowls with gold motif, best goblets, etc. (there had been a special party for the Princess Radziwill which could not be put off), and staggered to the swing doors, guiltily conscious of an extraordinary attempt at 'overloading'. My luck did not hold: the load slipped, and crashed to the inlaid stone lounge floor. Our 'management' was on me at once, but he suddenly pulled himself back, clenched his fists and walked away. That was the best and most expensive smash I have ever witnessed. Two days earlier the *tronc* would have been docked at least £20 and I should have been in the 'dog-house' with the staff for the rest of the season.

As it was, I became a most important member of the staff.

Factotum

I was stillroom assistant from 6 to 7 a.m. Floor waiter (in charge of one floor of forty rooms), 7 to 9 a.m. Breakfast in floor service; then washing up 9 to 10 a.m. Head silverman (smalls), 10 to 11.30 a.m. Butter-pat-maker, 11.30 to 12 a.m. (The stillroom was too hot for this, being in the kitchen, and ice had to be brought up from the valley 'if and when'.) Station waiter *salle à manger*, 12.30 to 2 p.m. Lunch, 2.30 p.m. The restaurant had been shut after the strike. Teas, 4 p.m. Supper, 6 p.m. Station waiter, 6.30 to 8 p.m. Lounge duties till midnight alternate nights, but every Saturday to 1 a.m. on dance nights.

Most afternoons when on *garde* duty from 3 to 4 p.m. I used to lie on two chairs in the dining-room and have a good old sleep. The high altitude and very long hours must have affected me, for my nose bled a lot during the next fortnight. My salary was still 30 Swiss francs per month.

This state of affairs lasted two weeks, until raw factory hands came to help with the chores, and a few cooks, waiters, and waitresses were found in the larger towns. The hotel remained full and the visitors took the part of staff and seemed quite to like waiting on each other.

One anecdote: Our head stillroom maid was the terror of the establishment well before the strike. The thirty waiters and twenty cooks—even Chef himself—were afraid of her. A grandly built woman of about forty-five, tall, thick-set, with dark hair, of Swiss-Italian origin, her tongue was the most viperous of any women I can remember. Her education was such that slang certainly predominated.

A few days before the strike, a waiter, feeling more exasperated than usual at being kept waiting, lost his temper, and shouted at her, '*Espèce de sale-vache—depeche toi salou.*' The balloon was pricked. The good woman collapsed, whimpering, 'Me an old cow?' We had peace after that—and thank heavens she did not join the strike.

Ten days later the season began to slacken. I had had a good three months' experience in glorious mountain surroundings. I left on 25th August for Biarritz. My *tronc* money was satisfactory, and an apparently grateful 'management' doubled my total salary.

These reminiscences may show the would-be *stagiaire* the fun and experience that awaits him if he gets abroad. Even in these days, with strict one-year exchange permits, the same type of experience can be had by a good mixer. My work at Villars was not so very impossible, and has remained in my memory above the happenings of the last twenty years—even above the incidents of air raids. Youth is impressionable. Abroad one learns, firstly, self-reliance—you are working alone in a foreign country; secondly, self-confidence—you must make the effort to speak a strange language; thirdly, self-application—you can learn and absorb all the tricks of the trade which are of vital use in after-life; lastly, a way to handle emergencies.

I have told half my strike story—from the staff angle only. Suffice it to say that that hotel continued full on practically no staff for two weeks. I learnt the reactions of visitors to management and visitors to loyal staff. I had the experience and opportunity afforded few, and I learnt how to handle certain eventualities by practical experience.

✳

I left Switzerland, via Geneva, at about 7.30 that night, *en route* for Biarritz (thirty-six hours away), where my next job as *commis de restaurant* awaited me at the Hôtel du Palais—one of the most fashionable, expensive, and best-run hotels in France at that time.

My haphazard journey calls for some comment. I travelled second-class—a little luxury I afforded myself, as I had earned good Swiss francs, which were 23 to the £1, as against the French at 170 to the £1. After dinner on the train, I reached Dijon about 11.30 p.m., and, being without lodging, decided to sleep rough and save my money. So I slept—or, rather, inhabited —the station waiting-rooms and the platforms until about 6 a.m. Now, for those many in our industry who are not aware of the night schedule of a main station, some of the activities will be of interest. Firstly, all the rats come out of their corners and play about in quite large numbers. Secondly, a lot more trains run by night than I had imagined, chiefly goods. But the most interesting experience was to see the great European long-distance trains come in.

Night Trains

Dijon is the first stop from Paris for trains going to Switzerland and Italy, and also the Côte d'Azur. At Dijon engines are changed. For a young man with all night on his hands, the spectacle was most instructive—even exciting. To the uninitiated, I would state that the trains to Nice and Monte Carlo are the most fascinating, on account of their near timing. The Train Bleu is the first to arrive—somewhere about 2.15 a.m. The sleeping-car conductors get out and have a little fresh air and a chat, some having a cup of coffee from a small trolley which appears from nowhere in case a hot drink or mineral water is required. Meanwhile, the enormous brute of an engine is panting up in front, waiting to be uncoupled. These large French engines really do pant, as if they had run a long race—which in fact they have. Their very considerable dimensions are enhanced by the shallow platforms on the Continent, so that one's head does not reach to the top of the driving wheels.

A new engine takes its place, and the train is off, to stop only at Lyons and Marseilles. The Blue Train is hardly out of the station, and the rear-lights are still showing in the distance, when the second express comes in on the same rails, carrying sleeping-car passengers direct from England via Calais. Following quickly are the Paris-Nice Express, and the Paris-Nice Rapide, so fast and near behind each other that they are assigned different lines. In under half an hour all four trains are off, speeding south. Now, this up-to-the-second timing is all the more remarkable if one has travelled Paris-Dijon in one of these trains, for Dijon lies in a hollow, and the trains have a downhill grade for several miles before coming to rest at Dijon. Their speed down these last few miles is well in excess of 70 m.p.h., yet accidents do not seem to happen. Not at that spot, anyway.

The Orient Express comes through later and has no need to make up time, as it is on its outward journey. It usually reaches Istambul fifteen to twenty hours late, according to the weather, the number of bandits about in what is now Yugoslavia, and the temperament of the engines east of Italy. This is no exaggeration. I have boarded the Orient Express, due at Lausanne at 11.15 p.m., at 2.45 a.m. The train is often eight hours late at the Italian border. It 'makes up' two-thirds of an hour across Switzerland, and in France it plugs along at Heaven knows what speed—to arrive in Paris a mere half-hour late, around 8.30 a.m.

Dijon-Bordeaux in those days of 1920 was a bad cross-country run, with only one good connection a day and very many miles of one-way track.

Runaway Trains

The train left early at about 7 a.m., if I remember—but that is of no interest at all in comparison with being a passenger in a runaway train. For this train actually got out of control. To reach Bordeaux, one has to cross France from east to west and over the Massif Central, which is the backbone of the country. We climbed and climbed—not steeply amongst mountains, but steadily through sunlit fields and freshly-cut corn, for many miles on a one-track line. At about lunch-time, we came to a junction with a double set of tracks—obviously the top of the pull. We started to go down on a long down-grade of, I should say, at least

twenty miles, and in the process we naturally gathered speed.
No one was alarmed until the carriage started swaying and the
wheels bumped from side to side against the rails. We came to a
curve. We went round it with no braking at all. The engine
began to whistle—not normally, but frantically. Everyone began
to look at each other; we fiddled with our hands, shuffled our
feet. We all had the same idea of a nasty, horrible crash. We
felt shut-in, hopelessly helpless. We had that feeling of thrill
one gets when seeing a runaway train at the cinema. But this
was not the cinema!

The gradient eased and we seemed to be going slower, and
fortunately were on a straight piece of line—straight for miles
apparently, as the French tracks so often are. I know all this
because I volunteered to look out of the window. We went
slower and slower with no signs of brakes being used. Then we
ran through the medium-sized station at the bottom of the one-
way track. We crawled on, to stop 50 yards past the platform.
Eventually, another engine was put on and we got to Bordeaux
at about 10 p.m. I walked around Bordeaux and had a snack at
a café. Again I watched the rats in the *Salle d'Attente*, as it was
not worth wasting money on a bedroom because I had to be up
again by 5 a.m.

Bordeaux Station was not so interesting; only the Madrid-
Paris train aroused my curiosity at 2.30 a.m. There are more rats
at Bordeaux than at Dijon, and people—poor like myself—fed
them with bits of bread from their paper parcels. I slept a little,
caught my early train—the Madrid Express—and eventually,
with one further short change, reached Biarritz about 7 a.m. I
hired a one-horse *fiacre*, loaded my trunk, and told the driver
to take me to the Hotel du Palais. He looked at me, and said
in hardly understandable Basque *patois*, 'Say, you're not the
King of Spain.' I was taken aback; he was right: I was *not* the
King of Spain. I saw my mistake and quickly added, 'Employees'
entrance.' He grinned and moved off.

King of Spain

After this long digression from Switzerland to Biarritz, it is
time I got back to the hotel atmosphere. Some of the waiting

staff were just coming on duty when I arrived. A young English-man accosted me with 'Better find yourself a room before they're all gone. This place is lousy with people now the King of Spain is here'.

This sounded friendly enough, so I parked my trunk and went to several addresses he had given me. After a long walk, mostly uphill, I found a small room and paid 50 francs deposit. It was a long walk, but anyway I had a bed. I walked back to the hotel.

My arrival had been reported, and who should I find in the pantry on my return but Mr. Cigolini himself, the General Manager, asking where the devil I had got to. I was greeted with a clap on the back and 'Here, my boy. There's a bed for you up top—sharing with the other English youngster.' (Mr. Cigolini, General Manager of Claridge's, London, was in Biarritz for some years before returning as General Manager to the Dorchester, London. He has retired now.)

Despite my fatigue of the last two days, I was told to report to the restaurant Manager for lunch, and was assigned to an Italian station waiter. Owing to the intensely busy season and the shortage of trained waiters, each *chef de rang* was assigned two *commis*.

This lovely restaurant, holding over eighty tables, faces the Atlantic rollers, which break in with a thunderous roar, the waves being much larger than anything we see in England.

The place was packed to the last inch. No wonder Mr. Cigolini wanted everyone on duty, for he was stretching his staff to a dangerous degree—and he knew it. Everything was *à la carte*, and to give an idea of the movement, four restaurant clerks and one cashier had their work cut out to keep up with the bills. Remember, this was 1920, and France was hardly out of a war. Staff were difficult to get, and consisted of French, Italian, and Spanish waiters. The kitchens were more adequate, the cuisine excellent, and the cooks ample for the job. The total brigade was capable of the 100 tables on gala nights, plus the floor service (which I never saw during my sojourn).

Of course, King Alphonse XIII was the attraction. I quickly spotted him sitting at a corner window-table overlooking the sea. More than half the tables in the room were regularly occupied

by Spanish nobility, who had lost nothing at all by remaining
neutral during the war.

I soon discovered a third Englishman, the table waiter to the
King of Spain. He had been at the Hotel du Palais for years, and
had settled down in Biarritz with his family.

Royal Waiters

Imagine my surprise when the restaurant Manager came to me
after my fourth day as twin *commis* on a station. He was in a
terrible temper. 'Here, you Englishman. Get on that station
with Charlie.' I nearly collapsed, and started to stutter that I did
not consider myself a very polished waiter yet. 'Shut your mouth
and do what you're told. We've had enough trouble in that *sacré*
corner.' I reported for the dinner service with Charlie. I asked
him what the matter had been. He laughed. 'His Majesty likes
speaking English. You see, his friend with him is American. He
hates changing languages in the middle of a sentence, so to
speak. Well, his eyes were fair flashing this morning when that
French *commis* did not understand. And they say us old English
are no good as waiters. Reckon we've got the plum job here,
anyway.'

So a partly-trained Englishman, with his English *chef de rang*,
took over. My job was more of a *commis debarrasseur*, for Charlie
did all the serving in old English footman style.

We only had the one table when the King was dining, and
would give a hand with the station next-door when His Majesty
left the restaurant. But this one table was not child's play, for
often very distinguished guests would be invited and six to eight
covers would be called for. On those occasions, I would shakingly
pass round the vegetables. (In French service the waiter passes
the dishes with one hand behind his back, and lets the visitor
help himself.) The heavy dishes were not exactly the easiest things
to handle, and I would come staggering up from the kitchen
with my eyes just showing over the top of the pile. Fortunately,
most of the others made way for me.

There is a great thrill to be had going to the kitchen on these
occasions. As I entered, I passed the queue of waiters lined up for
their orders, and went straight up to the *maître des cuisine*—no

aboyeur for me. He would call out: '*Sa Majeste le Roi—envoyez la selle de veau Orloff—tiens toi—tes epinards sont prets? chaud-laisse moi gouter. Et les pommes Macaire la bas. Patissier!*'

'*Oui.*'

'*Sa Majeste, les poires Belle Helène, en dix minutes, sont prets?*'

'*Entendu.*'

Chef would then personally 'load me up', so as not to have an accident *en route*. I need not say that a *selle de veau Orloff*—dressed and garnished—is a full one-man's load, without the vegetables.

Once I brought up a lovely *faisan à la Smitane*. The King looked at it: 'Take it away, my boy. Bring us some cold ham and cold beef—and don't forget, plenty of aspic jelly. Oh, and a *salade Nicoise*.' That is about the only time he actually addressed me.

Cashier

The King of Spain was my downfall, however. As all waiters, good, bad, and even indifferent, like myself, I used to enjoy the Royal food. I could not get any *faisan à la Smitane*, I remember, as it had to be replaced, and therefore returned to the kitchen untouched. But the *selle de veau Orloff*, and other dishes, were amongst the best food I have ever eaten—and I suppose I have eaten my fair share of banquets by now.

To cut a long story short, I went down with the colic. My room-mate brought me all sorts of things to share, which I felt like throwing out of the window. (I could not have done so, in any case, as they were covered with mosquito muslin.) After two days of griping pains, which bismuth and arrowroot did not cure, the colic suddenly left me. I suspect the change of climate to hot Biarritz, plus my Royal diet, caused my indisposition.

On the third day, I looked about me. I saw the advertisement in the local paper for a bull-fight at Bayonne for that afternoon. That was just the tonic I wanted. I sneaked out, imagining myself unseen, and took the local long-distance tram to Bayonne, some kilometres away. The number of bulls I saw killed and the number of old hack horses I saw gored to death is not for this chapter.

I was just nicely back in the basement when the staff doorman called to me, '*Le patron te demande petit—ou est ce que tu a ete?*' My luck was out. I tapped timidly at the door marked 'Direction'. I was informed that if I were well enough to go all the way to Bayonne to see a second-class bullfight, I was well enough to work. As I was liable to colic, I had better stop being a waiter, and report for dinner to the restaurant cashier department in one hour's time. (It was not put quite so nicely to me, but it boiled down to that.)

I reported in one hour's time, and was told to take over the cash. This rather surprised me, as it was a very busy and responsible job, involving a turnover of up to 50,000 francs a meal (about £7 10s. per 1,000 francs). One of the others 'showed me the ropes' for the first night, and I soon found that I had landed a most unpleasant job. The late cashier had been embezzling funds, paying 100 francs short in change, etc., and been caught when it became a little too frequent. The other three were obviously in with him, but were afraid to proceed in a share-out with a strange Englishman. I was not popular.

The experience, however, was of great value. I can now put my finger on almost any leakage of cash by looking for the tricks. Anyhow, today improved accountancy has stopped many of the old abuses.

Own Money

Only in the France of 1920 had one the permission—through force of necessity—to make one's own money. At that period, each *départment* (county) was responsible for its *petite monnaie*, and issued its own tender in 5- and 10-franc notes (9d. and 1s. 6d. approximately), but this was almost unobtainable. Most of this note issue was not valid between one *départment* and the next, so one had to be very sharp in accepting money from waiters on the payment of bills. Sums below 5 francs frequently occurred, and my predecessor had recourse to postage stamps for small change. Naturally, the waiters used to get any old stamps (sometimes even used ones would do if they were fingered enough) and try to pay them in for cash. This had caused a lot of wrangling, which I had previously noticed at the cashier's desk. I did not understand the cause at the time.

I stopped all stamp-swopping, and was nearly lynched for it by the waiters. My fellow cashiers stood up for me on this occasion, as they knew the abuse. Instead, I took the bull by the horns and went further by issuing my own money for anything under 10 francs. The 20-franc Banque de France notes were fairly plentiful. Even up to 10 francs only could easily mean up to 800 francs 'out' at a meal-time. Mostly these chits were left on the table as tips for the waiter, along with other larger money. They found their way into the *tronc* box and were redeemed at the end of each day when the head waiters reckoned up. They had to return them, several at a time, for me to be able to pay out in bank-notes. I think even the head waiters quite liked this arrangement. After a few days, I was sent for by Mr. Cigolini again. What was all this 'Goring's Bank' he was being told about by visitors? I explained my system. The *tronc* head waiter was sent for. He approved of it also. I was dismissed 'the presence' with a twinkling remark: 'I see you've got a little brain after all.'

On gala nights the congestion round the service doors and the cash desk was so great that I was moved to a different corner in the restaurant. Away from the others, I was more at the mercy of the waiters with 'Here, give me change for 1,000 francs. I'll bring the bank-note later.' In my proper place, I could handle that talk by shouting back and refusing, but in a fairly prominent place in the restaurant I was a more easy prey, for I could not shout and refuse as before.

Uneasy Europe

However, my vantage-point was most entertaining, and as my cashing-in of bills naturally came after people had dined, I had plenty of time to look round. At one of these galas, a certain very pretty and elegant youthful Spanish princess sat down to dinner in a most daring dress. It came as high as her waist—she carried a white open-net shawl—with a beautiful black Spanish shawl loosely flung over her shoulders. The *Gazette de Biarritz* fashion article described her the next day as 'That charming and attractive Princess was conspicuous for her perfectly shaped figure'.

The period of which I have written was a very unsettled time in Europe. Mussolini was collecting his forces for his ultimate

L

march on Rome, and many of the young Italian waiters were eagerly awaiting 'the day'. Mostly Fascist airmen, they were a dare-devil, fiery clique who kept together as a gang and did not get on with the Spanish contingent, who were from 'over the border' (fifteen miles away) for the season. One morning before the service, two waiters, one Italian, one Spanish, started a row. The Italian had taken one spoon off a laid-up table on the Spaniard's station. The Spaniard had his stiletto out at once, ready to stab: the Italian raised a large carving fork. Fortunately, the whole brigade was in the room at the time, and they were separated before any blood was shed. The Spaniard was immediately allotted a station in a different part of the room. Such were the sudden anxieties of the excellent head waiter—alert for trouble the whole time

My six weeks in Biarritz were most enjoyable. The bathing from the sandy coves—reminiscent of Devon—was excellent. The beach, the countryside, the firework displays, and the Carnival are all part of the memories—even the Casino, where I could only afford to play 'Boule'.

Again these pages have been penned without recourse to notes or diaries, which shows what joy a 'student-employee' can get out of a year's 'hard work' in Europe.

*

As many of us remember, Germany was in a pretty poor state after the 1914-18 War. Having already worked in hotels in Switzerland and France, I decided to earn my living in Germany and learn the language at the same time, which—as we all know in hoteldom—is one of the advantages of our profession.

In Dresden in 1921, however, I found things were not as easy as I had expected, despite my previous hotel experience in different parts of hotels on the Continent. Be it said that I was prepared to take a position as *commis de rang* or as control clerk. Even influence could not procure a job. Germany was the first country in Europe to enforce a ban on foreign workers, owing to the unsettled state of their country and the unemployment then rife.

I therefore decided to spend six months in Dresden with a private family, and use my father's allowance (£10 per month) for this purpose. This sum, about £2 10s. per week, I gave to a

Professor von Schleiben in return for board, lodging, and tuition in the German language. The von Schleibens lived very modestly indeed in the suburb of Radebeul, about twelve kilometres from the centre of Dresden. They occupied a small flat (no bathroom) in a 'select' street of gentlefolk in that delightful township. Along with most other people, I had to frequent the public bath-house about a mile away. The food was frugal in the extreme. We rarely had meat, but lived on beetroot soup, lentil soup, black rye bread (which I, fortunately, like) and vegetables. No butter— just *ersatz* fats on the bread. I mention this, as von Schleiben's brother had been War Minister of Saxony for eight years before and during the 1914-18 War, so that the difference in the scale of living must have been most marked in his case. Like so many unfortunate people of those times, the von Schleibens were ekeing out an existence and trying to be cheerful about it.

The Germans are very thorough, and I presume their children take their lessons more quickly and more thoroughly than we in England. I was taught well, kept my exercise and note-books in order, but did not learn or retain the terrible *der, die, das* of the German basic grammar (masc., fem., neuter). As a result, my professor was constantly scolding me for non-application.

The more I became discouraged the more I availed myself of the excellent suburban train service into Dresden. I travelled fourth-class, which was very cheap, and the local farm-wives, labourers, etc., were most interesting, even if their particular form of German was hardly understandable. It became plain that my professor's means were extremely limited, even with my contribution.

Extra Waiter at Dresden

Going to Dresden more frequently meant that I had to pay for my own meals. This, in turn, reminded me that I was really an out-of-work waiter. I had previously visited several of the better hotels in Dresden for a full-time job, as I mentioned above, with no results. So now I returned to see Herr Ronnefeld of the Hotel Bellevue, Dresden, one of Germany's six best hotels at that period. On my father's recommendation, I had tackled the famous Herr Dir. Ronnefeld previously for a full-time job, which he had reluctantly refused me on the grounds of *Arbeit-serlaubtnis* (working permit) difficulties. Herr Ronnefeld had been at the Bellevue for many years and was world-famous in his time. His twinkling blue eyes, snow-white hair, and immense, square-cut white beard made him a character.

On this occasion he received me, twinkled at me, wagged his beard and decided that there was no law against employing extra waiters 'as and when——' I therefore became an extra waiter about three days a week, mainly at week-ends. Soon afterwards I left Professor von Schleiben for a nicer room in a much better quarter in the middle of Dresden. I considered this a wise step, as I had friends in Czechoslovakia who asked me to visit them for the winter sports on several occasions. On one occasion I left Radebeul in the morning for the main station in Dresden, hoping to catch the only train to run out of that city for five days, owing to a railway strike. You can imagine my temper when I found I had forgotten my passport, and had to return and wait almost a week for the strike to be settled. On another occasion I biked up the very pretty River Elbe, mountains and all, to take a steamer from Pirna to Tetschen (Czechoslovakia), only to be told that I could not take my bike. As the frontier was only half-way to my destination, I reluctantly returned over the mountains, a very hot and bad-tempered young man.

During my stay in Germany my total expenses for six months did not exceed £30. This was due to the inflation of the German currency.

Internal prices did not rise so fast as the external exchange rate, so that I was able to obtain 750 to 1,000 RM. per £1. I bought a bicycle and a portable typewriter. I wrote articles for the old *Caterer*, under Mr. Bourne-Newton. I had many, many evenings dancing at the better places (Oh, yes, I admit to a girl-friend—it's the best way to learn a language), and, after selling my bicycle (which was not exportable to Czechoslovakia), I had spent £30—taking my extra waiter's duties payments into account.

Czechoslovakia

New countries south of Saxony had been formed by the 1919

Peace Treaty, when Austria-Hungary was divided into Austria (mainly Vienna), Yugoslavia, Hungary, and Czechoslovakia. As a person who lived and worked in this unworkable split of a nation, I was able to judge the disadvantages of that particularly bad peace treaty.

The old Austria-Hungarian unit certainly contained many disrupting elements. For example, Hungary grew the grain and supplied the eggs, poultry, and game. Bosnia supplied the tobacco and other—chiefly cereal—products. Bohemia (Czechoslovakia) was the industrial section, providing glassware, china, coal, steel, etc. Vienna was the central sales depot. With the break-up of this empire, which was only due to decadent governments, these four sections were made separate nations, with the usual unnecessary Customs controls, tariff duties, etc. The area of the old Austria-Hungarian Empire has never recovered from this split-up and, as we all know, they have—by their enforced, small and feeble efforts—been unable to counteract the ' Big Power' demands made on them from 1920 onwards. In other words, Vienna, as a city of 2,000,000 people, was too big a commercial centre to carry its henceforth very limited sales market. It was like a head without a body.

Czechoslovakia, the industrial sector without a head, found a good substitute in Prague, the ancient Bohemian capital, and became prosperous on industrial exports. In 1921 the Czechs were just finding their independence and taking it seriously. If one spoke German in Czechoslovakia one was not answered. However, if one spoke French or English one was answered in German—as a sign that the person asking the question could not speak Czech and allowance had to be made for them.

My next job—at the Savoy-Westend Hotel at Carlsbad—soon taught me this lesson, and my opening conversation was always in a non-Teutonic tongue.

At that time the foolish change-over of names did a lot of harm to the tourist traffic in Carlsbad and Marienbad, which had for centuries been known throughout Europe as famous cure resorts. To change these names suddenly to Karlovy Vary and Mariansky Laskni only complicated matters and did not improve hotel prospects *vis-à-vis* the British, French, and German clientele.

Taking the Cure

Such, therefore, was the state of the country I entered in 1922. Carlsbad was populated largely by German-speaking people kept down by a Czech minority who enforced their own language. From another point of view, a considerable amount of French influence was noticeable, especially in the matter of accountancy— of which more later.

I entered the Savoy-Westend Hotel as *chef de reception*. The hotel was not the biggest, but was one of the best—rating about fourth—in a town known for good hotels and international clientele. Seasonal, Carlsbad opens in May and closes in September. During these months, thousands of people visit the doctors and take the waters and mud baths in this unique resort.

Before taking a cure, visitors must see a doctor (fees strictly controlled) and have a prescription for the drinking of waters, as well as diet sheets. Many people are also prescribed mud baths.

As my shoulder was still troubling me, I had a course of mud baths, and most interesting I found them. One goes into a small room to undress. A big tub—shaped like a coffin and full of mud —is then wheeled in on railway lines and placed in position. With the help of an assistant, one gets into the bath and is covered with this hot, strong-smelling mud up to one's neck. Fifteen minutes is about the maximum one can remain immersed. All the time, the smooth mud surface is pulsing with one's heartbeats.

One wonders how one is to become dispossessed of this sticky, smelly mud. An attendant enters and helps one to stand up— and lo and behold, the mud slides off. Perspiration is so heavy that it forms a 'water-jacket' between the body and the mud.

This Carlsbad mud comes from a valley a few miles distant and is transported into Carlsbad. The deposit is vast and has been formed from an old deer burial-ground which is said to have existed for a thousand years. The thousands of wild deer which roam these forests used to come to this valley to die, in much the same way that elephants have their burial valleys. That this is true is borne out by the numbers of antlers found in the mud.

The Carlsbad thermal springs must be seen to be believed. There are several different kinds, from hot to cold. The main spring (*Sprudel*) is hot and gushes out of the earth, having to be controlled into the form of a strong fountain in the main thermal hall.

Carlsbad lies in a narrow, deep valley which entails much climbing on the part of the inhabitants, for from the famous Pupps Hotel at the valley end to the Savoy-Westend Hotel there is a difference of 200 to 300 feet. To reach the town valley to the Imperial on the opposite hillside is a job for a full-sized funicular. This vast Imperial Hotel was built by a member of the British nobility early in the century and is affectionately known as 'the Englishman's Folly'.

Hotel Economics

My duties as *chef de reception* were not arduous, although the hours were long. One very interesting system of paying tradespeople proved a small source of income, and I think the amount of energy expended walking up and down very steep hills justified the custom.

Most hotels live on credit all the winter and 'pay out' as the money comes in. The *chef de reception* is often the head cashier as well, and, instead of banking money, it was put in the safe, and every few days it was my business to go to shops selected by the management to pay back-accounts in cash. This entailed a very small discount for my courtesy in paying at all. The only ones to be kept paid up to date were the provision merchants. Other accounts were settled as the hotel got into the money-making months of July and August.

By far the best part of the cashier's duties, however, consisted of changing travellers' cheques into kronen. The Czech krone in those days fluctuated as much as 1s. in the £1 per day. This meant that by following the rise and fall on the money market and holding foreign currency for a few days a considerable financial benefit was available.

As in England, wages were paid every Friday. These wages were low, but the 10 per cent. system was in force, which made the pay packets up to quite a reasonable sum. The best scheme I have yet experienced was the gratuity system paid to chambermaids and valets. This department received 2 kronen per occupied bed per room per day (about 4d.), irrespective of room rates. This meant that in theory every room—expensive or cheaper—was worth the same amount of work to the chambermaid, who received the same gratuity added to the bill.

The system is easy to operate for the bill-office and is also a good control check between chambermaids and their occupied rooms, for, needless to say, every maid kept a check on her room occupancy to ensure her correct gratuity on pay-day. I have often advocated this scheme in England, but without result. I would even extend the system to the sale of wines, for it has always been wrong to charge a champagne drinker 10 per cent. in comparison with a customer who takes a cheaper wine, but receives the same amount of attention and service from the wine waiter. Surely a standard 'bottle tax' is preferable to a sliding scale, which can so easily upset a good client under the 10 per cent. system.

Meeting Jan Masaryk

Despite an extremely wet summer, many famous people visited Carlsbad for a cure for the first time since 1914. Train services were excellent and the roads were good. My highlight in reception work, however, was the visit of Jan Masaryk.

Jan Masaryk was the son of the President of the Czechoslovak Republic and was respected almost as much as his father. He spoke excellent American, having lived in that country for many years. His position was therefore very much like that of a crown prince. He was Czechoslovakian Ambassador to London, with his Embassy in Grosvenor Place, for most of the period between the two wars and, as we remember, met an untimely death as President of the Czechoslovak Republic in Prague.

Masaryk arrived at the Savoy-Westend Hotel one afternoon. A very nervous *chef de reception* asked him to kindly fill in an arrival form—or should the *chef de reception* fill in the form for His Excellency?

This is how the form was dictated to me:

> *Name:* Masaryk.   *Arrived from:* New York.
> *Pre-name:* Jan.   *(Beruf) Business:* Fond of the girls.
> *Age:* ——   *Signed:* Jan Masaryk (with a laugh).

This peculiar introduction led to a life-long acquaintanceship for, three years later, when at the Goring Hotel, Masaryk strolled in one day and, on seeing me, at once said, 'Weren't you in

Carlsbad a couple of years ago?' As a result, the big Czech industrialists, as well as Masaryk's personal friends, used to be sent to the Goring.

The first Bren gun came to the Goring Hotel from the Skoda works—before the War Office accepted it. This gun was a marvellous piece of mechanism, for the breech was housed in glass, so that the works of the gun could be seen in action. I therefore saw this gun before the War Office officials.

Officialdom in Action

About this time my parents arrived by car from England and stayed several days. One day we went for a drive into nearby Germany. We unwittingly overshot the Czech frontier station and were pulled up sharp at the German frontier station and sent back again. Smuggling was rife at that time and the Czech officials were very suspicious, and amazed that we had overshot their frontier. My father spent nearly an hour trying to persuade these officials of our innocence, and at last he came back to say that we were to be detained at the frontier post overnight and our car ransacked for dutiable goods.

I thought this was a little too enterprising on the part of these small-time, country Customs officers, so I strolled into the wayside office for the first time and asked for a telephone call to Mr. Masaryk at the Savoy-Westend Hotel, Carlsbad. Who was I? What did I want the telephone call for? How did I know where Mr. Masaryk was?

I said I had been drinking coffee with him only two hours before and that he would be very annoyed when he heard of this outrage. My bluff worked. With awed faces and voices we were escorted out of the frontier station and back to our car. Incidentally, Masaryk had left Carlsbad three days previously.

During my three months in Carlsbad I shared a room with the proprietor's younger son. This youth, about a year older than myself, had had a terrible experience during the war. Tall and good-looking, his hair was pure white. He had suffered from shellshock, been left on a battlefield, and had come back through Vienna in 1918, when the Czech nation had revolted. He was an enemy in his own Austria through his home connections in

Carlsbad. He spoke only Austrian. It had taken him six days to do an eight-hour train journey in a stolen train from Vienna, manned entirely by Czechs who, like himself, were fleeing from Vienna. Once well away from Vienna, they were left unmolested, but had no food for the 300 soldiers in the train. Fuel was obtained by cutting down trees on the track-side and burning green wood instead of coal. In a hilly country this is not a very easy way of locomotion.

My room-mate was most probably sharing with me for a purpose. His parents wanted him to 'open up' after two years of hardly speaking to anyone. His behaviour was very much that of the unfortunate Belsen and other camp prisoners of war of 1945.

We got on very well together and one evening—after about a month—he 'opened out'.

Apparently a shell had landed on a rock a yard or so from him, had spun round like a top and dropped to one side without exploding. He had been fascinated as by a snake and apparently had collapsed, as he remembered nothing more until he was in hospital. His hair had turned white within a few days of this unpleasant experience, and since that time he had kept within himself.

*

To come back to hotel subjects. Before the 1914-18 War nearly all the leading hotel managers were of German origin. The managers at the Ritz, Carlton, Piccadilly, Savoy, and Charing Cross hotels were German subjects, and very good hotel managers they were. At the outbreak of war in 1914 they fled the country to America, where they immediately found positions equal to those they had left in England. In my opinion, they were a great loss to the London hotel industry, for they really knew their job.

The unfortunate exit of the German hotel managers left the field open to the Italians, who proceeded to take over the more important positions in the larger London hotels. At the beginning of the 1939-45 War, the Italians—as enemies—were interned or sent home to Italy. Many of them (several hundreds) were drowned when the *Andora Star*, a liner chartered to take interned Italians (many hotel-men) to Canada, was sunk. As a result, in this decade, hotels in Great Britain are being managed today very largely by British managers.

In 1941 we had only one hotel and catering school in England —namely, the Westminster Technical Institute for Hotel Education, in Vincent Square, London, S.W.1. Today we have 134 technical colleges giving education in hotel subjects. I must claim a great deal of credit for this happy 'uplifting' of the hotel industry, as for two years I was Chairman of the Hotel and Catering Institute.

The Institute was founded by Mr. E. W. Collinson in 1943 and was known as the Catering Trades Education Committee. It later became the National Council for Hotel and Catering Education. On receipt of its Charter in 1949, it became the Hotel and Catering Institute, of which Sir Francis Towle was the first Chairman.

This is an institute on the same lines as other institutes (accountants, engineers, etc.), and is pledged not only to arrange technical college standard knowledge for the young, but also to grade hotel managers into various categories according to their knowledge and status in the industry. In its first three years (1943-6) the Institute graded 7,000 members into their different categories, i.e. Fellow, Member, Associate Member, and Student Member, as a backbone for our future ideas, which, of course, was entry to our profession by examination only.

We hope that in the future the hotel managers of British birth in Great Britain will all pass the Hotel and Catering Institute examinations. At the moment, after three years at a technical college studying catering subjects, students aged about twenty-one can pass the Associate Membership Examination of the Hotel and Catering Institute to show that they have reached a certain standard of knowledge. They then have to work for at least two years in the industry before they are allowed to use their letters, and before doing so their two years' experience in the industry is carefully checked by the Institute.

The next stage, having been confirmed in the A.M.H.C.I. status, is a five-year wait before they can apply for full Membership, which implies a standard of a good hotel and catering manager, aged by then about thirty-five years (minimum).

As Past Chairman of the Hotel and Catering Institute, I am personally very proud of the status we have achieved, not only towards our own industry, but also *vis-à-vis* the general public, Government departments concerned, and the educational authorities.

Many of us have worked very hard indeed to achieve our objective, and a young and rising hotel manager today uses the letters after his name in order to show his status in our industry when applying for a new position. We know that through training these letters imply knowledge of our industry.

We have thus created in ten years only an Institute capable of classification of ability by examination in craftsman* and managerial subjects on the same level as institutes representing other industries.

*

We are indeed proud that our industry earns more foreign currency for Great Britain than any other, and we are rated as the fourth largest industry, employing 750,000 people. One or two other industries may show higher export figures, but their *import* figures for raw materials must be reckoned with, which counts against their total net dollar earnings.

Our industry has no imports, as it is entirely a local (national) industry and needs no imports (except certain foodstuffs) to counteract its total hard-currency earnings.

As I have already mentioned, on the departure of the Italian hotel managers from this country at the outbreak of the 1939-45 War, we were left virtually with no first-class men. Hence our efforts in recent years to remedy our past failings and to provide progressive training in the hotel industry for British-born subjects. My above remarks do not only apply to managers; they apply also to waiters and cooks, the majority of whom in the past were of Continental origin.

Our lack of British waiters and cooks is still acute, but we are overcoming our difficulties at an astonishing rate. We have had for many years now an exchange scheme with the principal countries of Europe, by which semi-skilled cooks and waiters can enter England to take up hotel positions. This exchange

---

* Craftsmen examinations are for cooks, waiters, reception, book-keepers and control, and a student must have at least two craftsmen passes before he or she can sit for the Associate Membership Examination.

scheme also enables young Englishmen to do part of their training abroad and to learn the customs, languages, and habits in
hotels in the various European countries.

If I may coin an expression, the hotel business is 'universally
international'. In every country, hotels and inns are run according
to the needs, habits, and customs prevailing in their own particular area. But all serve food according to their national gastronomic preferences in the countries which are their homeland.
Their staff requirements are approximately the same.

This leads me to the International Hotel Association. With
Mr. Hugh Wontner, M.V.O. (Managing Director of the Savoy
Hotel Group), I have represented Great Britain on the Council
and the Executive Committee of this body since 1946, when the
I.H.A. was reconstituted from the pre-1939 basis of the then
existing bodies, the International Hotel Alliance and the International Hotel Association.

The International Hotel Alliance was a body of national hotel
associations, formed in 1920 to represent the hotel opinion of the
whole world from the viewpoint of national associations only.
Headquarters were in Paris. Each national association had one
vote in the International Hotel Alliance deliberations.

The International Hotel Association, known as the Inter-
nationale Hotelbesitzer Verein, had its headquarters in Cologne,
and accepted individual hotel members only. The 2,000 members
were actually very much more active and energetic than the
League of Nations type of organization which was represented
by the Alliance and had a much better and more friendly under-
standing of the day-to-day needs of hotel-men throughout
Europe.

My father was a strong and active member of the International
Hotelbesitzer Verein, and used regularly to attend their annual
conferences, always held in a different city. I can recall, and
actually attended, congresses in Lausanne, Budapest, Tripoli,
Cologne, Berlin, Rome, New York and elsewhere when my
father was on the Executive Committee and we had extremely
interesting times together between the wars.

The existing International Hotel Association is a combination
of these two associations, reformed after the war in 1946, with
two sections—one for national associations of each country, and
the other for individual hotel members from every country.

This international membership of individual members now extends to over 3,000 establishments in forty-seven countries.

The hotel business being entirely international, a central body for our industry is essential. We all know that the best hotels in every capital in the world follow the same pattern of bedroom accommodation and food. One can get the same menu in Tokyo, London, Paris, or New York. Whether this is desirable or not is beside the point.

Many individual members, however, represent smaller establishments in their own countries, and these are the members who like to meet at congresses in order to get to know one another and exchange experiences. Frankly, in the international hotel world we all know one another.

Since the formation of the International Hotel Association in 1946, we have held congresses for upwards of 1,000 people in Paris, Nice, London, Rome, Mexico City, Madrid, Brussels, New York and Dublin, at about eighteen-month intervals.

Apart from congresses, we have had Council Committee meetings, rather more interesting and intimate, for only about 120 people (ladies included), and have met in Athens, Scotland, Brussels, Paris, Nice, Stockholm, Copenhagen, Yugoslavia, India, Vienna, Berne, Washington, and elsewhere.

That is why I have under the glass table top in every bedroom at the Goring Hotel the following notice:

Mr. Goring is widely known to continental Hotelmen and has personally visited a large number of their establishments. He would always be pleased to assist guests in a happy choice of hotels almost anywhere in Europe.

*

Between the wars I was also very active in our special hotel managers' association, the Réunion des Gastronomes. This society, of about 160 of our best-known hoteliers, has very strict rules; and only those with undenied gastronomic ability are permitted to join. The society was founded in 1899, and holds a monthly supper, where very good food stimulates our conversation on current hotel matters. The great event of the year is the Annual Dinner (stag), the only occasion at which guests are invited, and even then the guests are closely screened as to their suitability. At this Annual Dinner the chef is expected to create a new dish, and the competition amongst the best hotel master chefs to prepare for this function is very keen, for these men realize that we know what we are eating and can appraise the amount of extra trouble and work which has gone into the preparation. I was President of the Réunion des Gastronomes for two years and am still on its Committee of Management after thirty-five years. In fact I am its oldest serving member.

*

I was also very interested in the Universal Cookery and Food Association, established about the end of the last century. This Association is to the public what the Gastronomes is to the professional. It consists of people in many walks of life, who are interested in cooking for cooking's own sake, and is formed of what I might call the housewives' section, strengthened by the best culinary experts in the country. It has the honour to be under Royal patronage, and, in fact, was one of the very few societies to have for many years two Royal patrons at the same time. These were the late Queen Mary and the Princess Royal. On the death of Queen Mary, Queen Elizabeth the Queen Mother graciously agreed to act as Patron.

The President of the U.C.F.A. has always been the acting Master of the Royal Household, which most probably accounts for our continued Royal patronage. Sir A. Keppel was the first President, followed by Sir Piers Legh and now Major M. V. Milbank, C.V.O., M.C., G.C.F.A. This, of course, accounts for my knowledge of the interior of Buckingham Palace, and the fact that I was permitted to have made, and present, the christening cake for Prince Charles, for I was Chairman of the Cookery and Food Association for two years just after the 1939-45 War.

*

One of my more important war side-lines was to be put in charge of blitz meals for the City of Westminster. This duty consisted of organizing the whole of Westminster to feed the public in case of major breakdowns in food supply due to bombing. It was actually a last line of defence in case of panic of the type which gripped certain cities in Germany. Westminster is by far the biggest 'feeding-out' centre in London. It includes the Strand, Charing Cross, Piccadilly, Soho, and Victoria as far as Knightsbridge. The area extends from the Hyde Park Hotel in the west to the Savoy Hotel to the East, and from the Thames at Vauxhall in the south to Oxford Street in the north. It contains very nearly all the hotels and restaurants of any distinction in London, a point which I had not realized when I came into the job.

Firstly, we divided our City of Westminster into seventeen sections, or wards, and put a warden in charge of each of them. Then headquarters supplied us with a list of all establishments in each section. These establishments varied from public houses and small cabman's pull-ups to Grosvenor House, the Dorchester, and the Savoy hotels. The problem was to ascertain the feeding capacity of Westminster. A warden, whose duty it was to visit *every* catering establishment in his area, was assigned to each of the seventeen wards. Each warden could have a deputy, or help—if he could find one—and only the warden for each ward was appointed by myself.

Fortunately for me, the scheme had been launched before I took over this immense task, but the donkey work still had to be done. The donkey work consisted of contacting every establishment, assessing their kitchen stove capacity, and explaining the scheme to the manager, landlord, coffee-stall-holder, or what have you, in charge.

Many of my voluntary wardens gave up and I had to find others, which was not a very easy task in wartime. To get around one ward took about six weeks of one's spare time, mainly during afternoons and evenings. I personally inspected every establishment in certain wards, comprising St. James's, Piccadilly, Vauxhall Bridge Road, and Pimlico. The number of establishments flabbergasted me, but they all had to be visited, their kitchens assessed, and their possible output computed. Many were rude at first and thought I was a Government snooper, sanitary inspector, income tax man, or food inspector, so it took a little time, in the first place, to be tactful and to explain that my job was a matter of national safety in case of major air raids, and that we should all help each other in a crisis, etc.

When I informed them that the food would be supplied free and all we were after were kitchen facilities, and possibly the staff to handle any cooking, I won the day, and all were delighted and indeed enthusiastic to show me their cooking facilities. Even today I can remember the types and varieties of kitchens in the West End of London, and I claim to have visited more catering kitchens than any other man in the world. They ranged from the Piccadilly, Savoy, Grosvenor House, Dorchester, Strand Corner House, etc., with a capacity of several thousand cooked meals per establishment (tinned food and bread quickly handled), to the small places capable of a maximum of between twenty and thirty meals only. The type of stove was also of the greatest importance, for gas and electricity was liable to be withheld or fail, according to bomb damage. Coal ranges were still the best, as they are independent of public services, which were liable to breakdown. Many establishments, on realizing how desperate the position might become, were prepared to put up field kitchens (temporary brick stoves, Army fashion). All these details were noted, and the final papers, still in my possession, are most impressive.

To keep up enthusiasm, we had local warden's meetings and 'get-together' meetings.

The actual scheme was that in case of a major breakdown in communications by bombing, many vehicles could reach certain rendezvous points with tea, coffee, bread, and possibly light meals. Meals could thus be assigned to each establishment for instant cooking and distribution to hysterical members of the public who had been bombed out of their homes. Allowing that the streets were not blocked by fallen houses and bomb rubble, the lorries could reach their rendezvous points by one street or another. Gangs of men could be standing by to transport the food stores—by hand, if necessary—to the various catering establishments ready to receive them.

This all sounds routine work, but the problem was to know which catering establishment was working. A bomb 400 yards away could fracture a gas main or cut a power line and throw the whole of a certain sector out of operation by either gas, electricity, or both. Hence our survey of catering equipment and how it could be used and what diversions of foodstuffs to another sector might be needed.

An actual incident will illustrate this unforeseeable problem. Several bombs fell in Pall Mall on certain large club premises and fractured the gas mains. An emergency call was made to the gas control to have these mains cut off at the road-control stopcocks.

Up St. James's Street and including Piccadilly—on higher ground—the gas was therefore also cut off, according to the position of the stopcocks. While my very valuable catering establishments in Clubland would perforce be cut off to my certain knowledge, I had no information as to how far the damage had gone and what gas was available at a higher level— say, at the Piccadilly Hotel (3,000 meals)—until a check had been made on the situation. It would, therefore, have been no good putting a food blitz meals lorry stationed in Piccadilly Circus if gas-main breaks had taken place even 800 yards away unless control stopcocks could cause the gas pressure to rise up from the Mall to Piccadilly (100 feet rise).

After several incidents of this nature, the gas companies decided to reorganize their system of gas control stopcocks to take in smaller areas and thus diminish the risk of fire by gas escapes. This major operation was one of the great benefits to the city in the blitz years from 1940-2, for today all gas mains have been stopcocked to cover smaller areas than before. Hundreds of extra stopcocks were put into the mains to achieve this object, so that today a major gas blow-out would effect only a minor section of houses around it. Actually, I still have the complete list of control check points in gas mains as finally built and established by the gas authorities. The system of gas mains control through the new basic flow of gas has been very considerably helped by the wartime emergency of new stopcocks. All our Fire Brigade modernization was made in 1941 to combat German bombs. I feel sure that if this fire threat on major lines had not arisen, we would still have the old fire engines of the past.

After all our efforts, our blitz meals services were never put into operation. Fortunately, bombing conditions in London never reached the 'action' limit, when our services might have been called upon. We had a near call on a big bombing raid just south of the Thames in Southwark: hundreds of people were killed in a sudden, concentrated raid and it looked as though our services would be called upon. However, local resources were used and the emergency was met.

If our resources had been called upon to any considerable degree, we, in Westminster alone, would have been able in 1941 to supply meals for 350,000 twice a day. This, I maintain, would have been a very considerable achievement, for the whole of London could not have been bombed in one night, and the suffering and confusion could therefore, have been carried by the one main feeding centre, Westminster. The actual feeding capacity with regard to blitz meals in the City of Westminster was more than double the facilities of the whole of the rest of London and outlying suburbs combined. That is why we concentrated on the Westminster area for our plans.

The blitz meals service was a very real and serious effort to help the London population should disaster overtake them. It was never used—thank Heaven—but the organization, on a full operative basis, was available.

Mr. I. M. Gluckstein, now Chairman of J. Lyons & Co., and myself did a long and weary job to get this blitz meals organization on to an operational basis. It would have worked, but, thank God, the bombing from the Germans never called for us to put the scheme into practice.

After the war was over we had a dinner at the Trocadero Restaurant. We congratulated ourselves on our achievement, but nobody else was there to praise us, for nobody else knew what we had done!

*

And so the second twentieth-century pre-war, war, post-war, cycle goes round. The hotel business has been in the throes of a boom for the last fifteen years, just as it was after the First World War, and the Goring Hotel has flourished to a greater degree than ever. Each year has seen a considerable improvement in turnover and each year we seem to have reached our maximum. Yet year by year this increase of business continues until, at the moment, it can almost go no further.

The secret surely can be summed up in the one word—individuality. Not necessarily the individuality of one person, but a team of people working as one individual unit.

Here the proprietor-operated establishment—provided the proprietor is really hotel-minded—proves its worth. The friendly atmosphere of a one-man business does not permeate the atmosphere of big chains of hotels, however efficiently organized and controlled. An essential part of chain hotels is 'control.' 'Control' implies a strict rule-of-thumb-no-deviation attitude, which covers the overall object of money-making for the large company concerned, but which allows little of the human element to enter into the picture. We say that the hotel industry is individualistic, by which we mean that every hotel or restaurant is run on slightly different lines according to the manager in charge. Thus we have no hard and fast rules except the fundamental laws of basic wages.

Trades unionism does not affect our British hotels, for no labour union can gain a foothold—thank heaven! Establishments and workers are independent—and what a blessed state of happiness this means to them and to us. No strikes—unofficial or official—very few disputes and an independent ability to change iobs summer or winter, to seaside or town, or to remain stationary, according very largely to inclination.

What can be more galling to a competent hotel manager than to have to take orders (virtually from a junior waiter), adopt certain rules and regulations to comply with some autocratic and non-understanding trades union—as happens in France, Switzerland and Germany.

These union methods, though suitable to standardized industries which turn out goods to specification, would only standardize hotel custom, and what a terrible thing it would be to have everything uniform in every establishment. Even now people grumble about the 'sameness' of international hotels, and in my opinion they grumble with reason.

Remember, no two individuals in this world are alike, and no two people have lived exactly the same life. Of the thousands of millions of people in this world today, and in the centuries of the past, no two people have exactly the same history, the same environment, or the same sequence of experiences.

Trades unionism seems to try to regimentate factory workers into one pattern, at least within the confines of the factory. Hotels, however, should and must be run on individualistic lines—for are we not all individuals in the true meaning of the word?